T0366520

SHAKESPEARE AND THE COCONUTS

on post-apartheid
South African
culture

COCONUTS

SHAKESPEARE AND THE COCONUTS

on post-apartheid South African culture

NATASHA DISTILLER

WITS UNIVERSITY PRESS

Published in South Africa by:

Wits University Press
1 Jan Smuts Avenue
Johannesburg
2001
www.witspress.co.za

Edited by Inga Norenius
Cover design and typesetting by Farm Design www.farmdesign.co.za
Printed and bound by Ultra Litho (Pty) Limited

Contents

Acknowledgements

My work on Shakespeare and South Africa was first developed in *South Africa, Shakespeare and Post-colonial Culture* (Lampeter: Edwin Mellen Press, 2005).

I would like to gratefully acknowledge the anonymous peer reviewers for Wits University Press, whose rigorous engagement with the original version of this book helped to improve it immeasurably. I thank them for their time, input, knowledge, and collegiality.

Permission to publish reworked versions of the following journal articles is gratefully acknowledged:

Taylor and Francis Group for 'The Mobile Inheritors of any Renaissance' – *English Studies in Africa* 51.1 (2008): 138–144; 'English and the African Renaissance' – *English Studies in Africa* 47. 2 (2004): 109–124; 'Begging the Questions: Shakespeare in Post-apartheid South Africa' – *Social Dynamics* 35.1 (2009): 177–191.

University of Delaware Press for '"Through Shakespeare's Africa": "Terror and Murder?"' – *Shakespeare's World/ World Shakespeares*, eds Richard Fotheringham, Christa Jansohn, and R.S. White (Newark: University of Delaware Press, 2008), pp. 382–396.

Ashgate Publishing Group for 'Tony's Will: *Titus Andronicus* in South Africa 1995' – *Shakespearean International Yearbook*, eds Graham Bradshaw, Tom Bishop and Laurence Wright (Farnham: Ashgate, 2009), pp. 152–170.

Cambridge University Press for 'Shakespeare and the Coconuts' – *Shakespeare Survey* 62 (2009): 211–221.

Thanks to Stephen Francis and Rico Schacherl for the *Madam & Eve* cartoon – *Mail & Guardian* 30 November – 6 December 2007, p. 33.

Grateful thanks to Ingrid de Kok for permission to use her poem 'Merchants in Venice' which was first published in *Terrestrial Things* (Kwela Books and Snailpress, Cape Town, 2002) and later re-published in *Seasonal Fires: new and selected poems* (Seven Stories Press, New York, 2006).

My thanks to Jennifer Poole for her sterling research and editorial assistance, to Julie Miller and Roshan Cader at Wits University Press, and to Inga Norenius for her editing.

Introduction

Ingrid de Kok's poem 'Merchants in Venice' addresses the relationship between rich, established Europe and its so-called high culture, and poor, entrepreneurial Africa. The poem offers ways to read the presence of Africans in this famous landscape. One of the poem's subtexts speaks to Africans' political, economic, and cultural rights, and the disavowal, refusal, or lack of their recognition. Ancient histories of exchange resonate with the globalised present, as the young men of De Kok's poem are saturated, not only in Venice's celebrated light, but also in relations of power that span time and place, and are imbricated with the markers of culture invoked by the poem's descriptions as well as by its title:

Merchants in Venice

We arrive in Venice to ancient acoustics:
the swaddling of paddle in water,
thud of the vaporetto against the landing site,
and the turbulent frescoes of corridors and ceilings,
belief and power sounding history
with the bells of the subdivided hour,
on water, air and all surfaces of light.

What have we Africans to do with this?
With holy water, floating graves and cypresses,
the adamantine intricacy of marble floors,
gold borders of faith, Mary's illuminated face

and the way Tintoretto's Crucifixion is weighted
with the burden of everyday sin and sweat,
while the city keeps selling its history and glass.

On the Rialto, tourists eye the wares
of three of our continent's diasporic sons,
young men in dreadlocks and caps, touting
leather bags and laser toys in the subdued dialect
of those whose papers never are correct,
homeboys now in crowded high-rise rooms
edging the embroidered city.

How did they get from Dakar to Venice?
What brotherhood sent them to barter and pray?
And on long rainy days when the basilica
levitates, dreaming of drowning,
do they think of their mission and mothers,
or hover and hustle like apprentice angels
over the shrouded campos and spires?

Into the city we have come for centuries,
buyers, sellers, mercenaries, spies,
artists, saints, the banished,
and boys like these: fast on their feet,
carrying sacks of counterfeit goods,
shining in saturated light,
the mobile inheritors of any renaissance. [1]

De Kok's poem brings to the surface what is hidden beneath
the beautiful veneer of European culture, 'the way Tintoretto's
Crucifixion is weighted / with the burden of everyday sin
and sweat, / while the city keeps selling its history and glass'.

Commerce and its patterns of exploitation, and the real lives of real people lived above, beneath, and within the layers of art and history that comprise the physical and cultural architecture of Venice, inform Europe's beautiful objects and invest them with a different meaning to their commodified claims to fame. The poem insists on this without reducing Europe's artistic accomplishments to instrumentalist objects of power and overpowering. At the same time, the poem makes visible the human struggles which belie any easy celebration of intrinsic worth. It brings history and politics into art. It also stakes a claim for what Africans are entitled to inherit from this history, by insisting that they have always been a part of the grubby, painful human living which makes high art, which enables it to exist as object and as artefact. Europe's art would not mean what it does without Africa, that is, without its exploited human and other resources, and its symbolic position in a global history and economy. With this acknowledgement, Africans' relationship to Europe's texts and treasures becomes participatory. At the same time, 'art', 'Europe', and 'Africa' are all located in the realities of daily life, within the dynamics of which each concept is constructed.

The poem allows for a discussion of the ways that people produce artefacts and ideas. Some of the most celebratory writing about Shakespeare can make it sound like we are products of Shakespeare's texts, which become ahistorical and unimplicated in politics and materiality. This book describes some of the ways Shakespeare's texts have been implicated in South African history, politics, and materiality. In addition, it explores how and why this history matters.

Let me say from the outset that while I am arguing against seeing Shakespeare's literary or philosophical influence in South Africa as proof of 'his' universality, I am not therefore arguing that 'he' has no 'authentic' place in South Africa. Indeed, the anxieties about authenticity and belonging raised by debates on Shakespeare are far more interesting to me than what I consider to be historically inaccurate and theoretically naïve statements that rely on essentialised versions of concepts such as 'culture', 'African', 'European'. De Kok's poem makes it clear that these ideas are always products of material history, of people's investments (financial and emotional), of complex human processes.

Shakespeare and coconut logic

There is a long tradition of South Africans appropriating Shakespeare, which goes back to the colonial mission schools. The nature of that appropriation is complex, and involves socio-political interactions and aspirations, including specific colonial, South African, incarnations of the dynamics of class mobility and modernisation, their relation to Christianity, to English as a language of social and therefore economic power, and to English Literature as a formalised field of study. South Africans who have entered into this tradition have been seen as selling out to a kind of colonial coconuttiness which enabled the entrenchment of a racist social system, or as transforming the master's tools in order to dismantle his house. However you want to read their behaviour, the fact remains that they read, loved, and used Shakespeare in their own lives and works. So Shakespeare has an African history, which is as African as any other aspect of the region's cultural development. To say this is to take a political stand, one which refuses to see colonial history and its aftermath as containable by binaries: coloniser/colonised, oppressor/oppressed, European/

African. I am not for a moment suggesting that the multiple violences of colonial history, the apartheid regime which it enabled, and the ongoing inequalities which are our legacy were or are in any way excusable. I am suggesting, as have many other cultural critics and anthropologists, that human interactions and the artefacts they produce are always complicated. To say that South Africa's history has always been a history of complicities and complex engagements and influences is not to ameliorate the racist, gendered, classed violence of the region. This book argues that exploring aspects of the ways Shakespeare has been used, appropriated, symbolised, and reproduced in post-apartheid South Africa is one way to begin to see the complexities and paradoxes of our national history. This is a particularly apposite argument now, as raced identities are increasingly reinscribed in public discourse, encouraged by the posturing of some of our leading politicians.

Many of our writers have appropriated Shakespeare. It is not a question of looking for a South African writer who is 'like' or 'as good as' or 'trying to be' Shakespeare. And it is certainly not a question of finding evidence of Shakespeare's universality in the fact of 'his' having been used by Africans. If we dispense with the too-easy answer of 'universality' (which is too easy not least because it is disingenuous), we can explore more interesting answers to the question, why was it *Shakespeare* these writers appropriated, and with whom we are still concerned in sometimes quite highly charged debates? This question draws us into a cultural history which teaches us about how cultural value is invested and perpetuated, bought and sold, if you like, as well as experienced and owned by individuals (think again of De Kok's poem). It also enables us to trace the power relations in English Literature as a field of study, and English as a language of social and political power, in our region. Looking at these processes, amongst others (such as the history of Shakespeare editing practices), enables us to see why the language of universal relevance is disingenuous, and to uncover its own political history and material investments.

Nevertheless, in response to the question, why is Shakespeare still important in South Africa today (or, more specifically, why did Shakespeare comprise an influence on writing in English in the region, or why do people still argue about Shakespeare's relevance)?, most people say, not least because it is what they have been taught at school, that Shakespeare's work is relevant to South Africa because his themes are universal. All people, after all, have issues with their parents (*King Lear, Hamlet*), or are jealous about something (*Othello*), or can relate to forbidden love (*Romeo and Juliet*), and so on. But all good literature is universal. The best will deal with human emotions that we can all relate to. How is it, then, that Shakespeare is the standard for universal humanity and not Chinua Achebe? More pointedly, why is Shakespeare considered universal and Chinua Achebe considered the spokesman for a specific culture?

If we leave aside the workings of colonial value systems obviously at play in the comparison between Shakespeare's universality and Achebe's tribal specificity, the answers to questions about why Shakespeare has become the embodiment of literary universality in English lie in specific material histories. These include the history of the British theatre in the seventeenth century, in the development of editing as a scholarly practice in the eighteenth century, and in the social dynamics of an education system developed during British colonialism in the nineteenth century, which is tied to English nationalism. It may seem that I am now saying that Shakespeare is indeed a colonial import. It is a short step from there to the assertion that his texts have no place in South Africa. This would put me in the camp of those who, like the Kenyan writer and activist Ngugi wa Thiong'o, would reject the effects of colonial history and seek to recover an authentic African literature or history or experience. What I want to make clear in this introduction, however, is that I find conceptualisations of culture (and the identities on which experiences of culture and tradition depend) as ever having been pure, as idealised, or as reclaimable, to be invested political and psychological fictions.

Over and above our South African Shakespearean tradition, there are other reasons to retain an interest in Shakespeare in post-colonial and post-apartheid South Africa. In the first place, all knowledge is relevant to all people, and for that reason alone Shakespeare belongs to us as much as 'he' does to anyone else. In the second place, Shakespeare has cultural capital that Africans are as entitled to as anyone else. In the third place, Shakespeare is a part of African experience. But these justifications rehearse recognisable positions in an old and, in my opinion, quite tired debate, which ultimately relies on the reinscription of colonial and apartheid binaries, where one is either 'authentically' African or able to access so-called European culture. As our own writers have indicated from at least Solomon Plaatje onwards, and as De Kok's poem also illustrates, this is a false binary. In post-apartheid South Africa, after all, isn't this kind of traditional coconut logic exactly what we want to be moving away from?

The term 'coconut' is one of several edible designations, including 'bounty' (from the American Bounty chocolate bar), 'topdeck' (a South African chocolate bar), 'apple', 'banana', and, of course, 'oreo' (from the American Oreo cookie), used to designate someone who, due to their behaviour, identifications, or because they have been raised by whites, [2] is 'black' on the 'outside' and 'white' on the 'inside'. [3] These terms are in operation in the UK, USA, South Africa, New Zealand, and China, amongst other places. The focus on 'acting' or 'feeling' 'white' in a range of communities across the globe points to the ongoing prevalence of white privilege as a structuring principle of our neo-colonial world. [4] The different terms also speak to the imbrication of racial profiling with personal identity, in that ethnicity is yoked to skin colour, which in turn is presumed to designate a fixed identity. 'Coconut' specifically, although used in South Africa to denote black people (most often with a particular kind of education which includes fluency in English and a media profile, as in 'coconut intellectuals'), has provenance elsewhere as a term for people considered 'brown', not 'black': Asians, Indians, Latinos, Filipinos. [5] In all places, used by those who are claiming access to an authentic blackness of whatever shade, the term has derogatory implications of inauthenticity, artificiality, and sometimes shameful or shameless aspiration. In South Africa, the appellation 'coconut' is currently in extensive circulation, and is closely tied to class mobility as indicated specifically through speaking a specific kind of 'white' English. [6]

This conceptualisation of personal identity is crude in its essentialising of blackness and whiteness, and reliant on notions of cultural authenticity. Assertions of cultural purity and their concomitant legitimations, invocations of tradition, are nostalgic and political, if powerful, fictions. This book intends to challenge the negative implications of the accusation of coconuttiness, while still retaining an awareness of the histories of power and overpowering which give the label its bite. It explores the workings of the notion of the coconut specifically in relation to a number of ways Shakespeare might be experienced in post-apartheid South Africa. In the end, I suggest two new ways of understanding coconuttiness, which offer new definitions that refuse the binary logic of the original meaning, without losing sight of the embodied experiences of living (with) race in South Africa today.

Overview

I begin with the past. In the first chapter I sketch the history of English and Englishness in the region, and place Shakespeare's symbolic English Literariness in context. I also focus on Solomon Plaatje as the first example of a (newly defined) South African coconut. I do this to suggest that his uses of Shakespeare allow us to explore the processes of cultural transformations, personal identification, and class complicities at work, in ways which point to the realities of colonial experience. These ways belie colonial and apartheid binaries, including constructions of Europe, and Europe's relation to its construction of Africa and Africans. This history also allows us to see the complex and ambivalent inheritances which are ours as South Africans, and which other recent work on English Literature, on modernity, and on their material processes in South Africa has illustrated. [7] Given Plaatje's lifelong commitment to achieving political and cultural recognition for black South Africans, calling him a coconut helps to begin to reformulate the charge of race treachery implicit in the term as it currently stands.

From positions within universities around the world, academics have been arguing for the last thirty years that Shakespeare's putative universal relevance is a creation of a colonial system which sought to entrench the culture of the coloniser and that Shakespeare's cultural solidity and textual stability are constructions of his editors in the first instance. Chapter two examines some of the ways the connections between

'Shakespeare' and a generalised 'Africa' have tended to be made. I argue that looking to claim the universal Shakespeare for this version of 'Africa' is indeed a reinscribing of a patronising dynamic which relies on a binary understanding of race and a problematic understanding of 'African' culture.

This construction of the relationship between Shakespeare and a version of Africanness in South Africa sets the tone for exploring other ways Shakespeare has been invoked since liberation to reinscribe the very values we should be moving away from. In chapter three I trace another instance of Shakespeare's incarnation as the epitome of an Englishness that is positioned against a constructed South Africanness, this time a 'white' South Africanness. In acclaimed expatriate actor Antony Sher's charting of his experience of staging *Titus Andronicus* in newly post-apartheid South Africa, I argue, the same old colonising dynamics are at work. Sher, I suggest, is an example of coconuttiness too – the old kind. His is a presentation of South Africanness as a veneer, and it relies on the binary logic of the traditional idea of the coconut.

In chapter four I explore another of the ways the universal Shakespeare is still very much in evidence in post-apartheid South Africa, in the arena where most of us who will do so, will encounter his texts – school. This suggests that the rich South African Shakespearean tradition exemplified by Plaatje's work (but including a host of other writers, mostly but not exclusively in English) is not being recognised or disseminated.

One of the many ironies of post-apartheid South Africa is the fact that this problematically universal Shakespeare animated a programme of African renewal. In chapter five I argue for recognising the relationship between the African Renaissance and Eng Lit (by which I mean to designate English Literature as a formal field of study), and therefore the inheritances of

English for South Africa, specifically in its implications for those of us in the economic and linguistic elite of the country. The African Renaissance, which depends in part on what Shakespeare has come to stand for in the neo-colonial world, uses this dependency to argue for a traditional Africanness. In its complex and contradictory cultural work, the concept of the African Renaissance makes clear that our post-colonial and post-apartheid present is constituted by loss and fracture. We must own this starting point, which goes right back to Plaatje, in order to explore our possibilities for the future, or we will remain stuck in the logic of our terrible past.

The African Renaissance was Thabo Mbeki's baby, and it is no coincidence that this most eruditely self-fashioned of presidents was saturated with Shakespeare in his public persona. In the final chapter, I suggest that post-Polokwane and Mbeki's spectacular fall from power, the familiar version of high-cultural Shakespeare now definitely stands for something un-South-African in the popular imagination. In the colonial and apartheid past, Shakespeare stood for empowerment in a socio-economic system dominated by 'white' culture. To know your Shakespeare was to contest your positioning as a 'native'. Recently, however, Shakespeare seems to have come to stand for something else. The changed meaning of Shakespeare is related to the charged meaning of English, as a language and as a coconut identity in post-apartheid South Africa. As material inequalities continue to worsen, and as English remains the necessary pathway to economic advancement even as our education system deteriorates, the coconut becomes a figure of privilege increasingly accused of rejecting and so betraying his or her African roots.

Reclaiming the coconut

In an article published in 2007, the same year as Kopano
Matlwa's novel *Coconut* won the European Union Literary Award,
Andile Mngxitama calls a new generation of 'influential young
people ... neither black nor white'. [8] Although they constitute
a numerical minority, he says, 'they are a cultural majority'.
Mngxitama accuses this generation of Africans of being agents
of colonialism along the lines of Fanon's mimic men, '"black
outside and white inside"'. He descries their lack of interest
in their own history, and accuses them of being 'agents of
whiteness' who will inherit the new South Africa and set the
terms for a denigration of blackness, including black languages.
While the political imperatives underlying this critique remain
important – the production of an economic elite when poverty
remains a dire issue, the lack of support for indigenous African
languages, the youth's relationship of disavowal to the country's
racialised history which allows inherited structures to perpetuate
unchallenged – what I wish to refute in this book is the binary
logic which continues to structure public discourse about who
and what South Africans can and should be in relation to each
other. Characterising this emerging elite as 'white' on the 'inside'
reproduces a version of culture as capable of being authentically
or inauthentically African, a version which is currently being
deployed by the very political leaders who continue to let us
down. It is also ignorant of the history Mngxitama wishes our
youngsters would own. Perhaps if we begin to teach a version
of South Africanness that is fundamentally coconutty, we can
recapture the interest of the generation emerging as inheritors
of that particular history. And I mean by this to remake the idea
or reclaim the image of the coconut: Mngxitama invokes the

commonsensical notion that a coconut is made of an outside and a differently 'coloured' inside.

My reclamation of the term is, of course, in part ironic and provocative. The coconut is useful as a psychologically loaded symbol, one which encodes racial histories and identity struggles. In arguing for using the icon anew, I am suggesting that its logic of outside and inside be refused, and that instead we celebrate what the charge of coconuttiness is trying to name in its derogatory way. As I will keep reiterating, I am not simultaneously arguing for a version of history which denies the oppression that was perpetuated in the name of racism, or the suffering that black people had to endure because they were black. That racialised past, and its consequences, are very much with us today. But I am arguing that there is also a version of South Africanness that has always existed, which cannot be captured by a binary logic, and which may be very productive of a way forward for our national imaginary. Because it is rooted in history, it is not like the anodyne rainbow nationhood that Mngxitama rightly objects to.

I use Shakespeare to demonstrate the genesis of and potential in our reformulated coconut possibilities. That this reclaimed coconuttiness has tended not to make it to our public performances, textual or political, is evidence of the ongoing power of the colonial and apartheid binary logic in which one is either/or: either authentically African, or European; either a purified and nostalgic version of black, or white (on the inside, or otherwise). As I argue in the final chapter, the ongoing power of this binary is reflective of very real ongoing inequalities which tend to remain raced, and of the existence of inherited structures of white privilege within which all South Africans have to try to make it. But at the same time, I also want to point out the ways in which discourses of authentic blackness and traitorous whiteness are easy political tools, which deny aspects of our history and our identities for expedient and dangerous agendas. These range from a murderous homophobia to a violent misogyny, to a form of political smokescreening, where colonial history is rhetorically deployed by leaders whose corrupt practices ensure they benefit from the system, the exploitative qualities of which they lay at the feet of white people.

Ultimately, I hope to make it clear that Shakespeare's cultural value is, in our context, a complex signifier. While in the course of the arguments made here I do argue for some of the implications of the fact that English Literature as a discipline, and Shakespeare as one of its foundational figures, are both colonial imports developed to be colonising tools, I am not suggesting that Shakespeare therefore has no place in post-apartheid South Africa. I invoke the idea of the coconut, not to endorse its reductive and contained notions of race and identity, but to challenge those ideas and to reclaim the image of the black person worked on by history through English. Perhaps some South Africans have always been coconuts – that is, have internalised and been formed by a relation with English – and we should start to understand coconuttiness as a legitimate identity. I cannot, according to the logic of my argument, call it an authentic identity, since the language of authenticity has been too often invoked in the names of a putatively pure Africanness or a whiteness in need of protection from contamination. But I am suggesting that the messy in-betweenness, the mixed-up inside-outsideness of the coconut trope may be a more accurate descriptor of what some South African subjectivities have always been, since the region first encountered English. Ultimately, I argue, what we in post-apartheid South Africa need to leave behind are precisely those colonial and apartheid binaries which fail to describe who and what we – that complex, fractured, differential South African citizenry – are and, more importantly, who and what we can be.

Who are 'we'?

> 'We' is a tenuously created category, stitched together with deep ambivalences of signification. May 'we' at least remember *that*, if nothing else. [9]

In the course of this book I will refer to 'us', South Africans. Given the diversity of people's experiences of nationhood and citizenship and the vast discrepancies in access to services, living and working conditions, and other class-, race-, and gender-inflected differences of experience in this country, it is important to specify that the 'we' to which I refer cannot be taken to mean all South Africans. Indeed, the history of access to literacy in English in this country, and particularly to exposure to canonical English Literature taught in the traditional way, has always been class-inflected for most South Africans. Those with access to mission-school education, in colonial times, were by and large the ones who became writers in English. Under apartheid, Bantu Education inflected English Literature teaching very differently for most black South Africans. So in the first place, 'we' are those South Africans of a limited range of classes and literacies that enabled us to encounter English, Eng Lit, and Shakespeare, in ways which made it possible to enjoy and sometimes own the literature, and to profit from fluency in English.

Secondly, although most white South Africans will not have a personal identity investment in the idea of African tradition or reclaimed Africanness (although some do – presumably those who have been called to become sangomas, for example, have at least partial access to a personal sense of African tradition), many of us are invested in the discussions about Africanness. From commercial and tourist performances [10] to nationalist constructions, to contestations over who qualifies as an African (after centuries of disavowal, many whites are now anxious to claim an African identity of sorts), personal identities with regard to Africa and Africanness are helping to form and formulate post-apartheid identity in general. 'We' can then be South Africans of any of the 'races' who have encountered Shakespeare via institutions which disseminate Eng Lit, with all the access, and subjection, to systemic power (gendered, social, economic, and, eventually, political) this implies.

'We' also exist in a time and space variously called post- or neo-colonial, and/or post- or neo-apartheid. These designations are not uncontested. It is true they are politically simplistic given, not least, the diversity of experiences of the past and present in this country that makes a definition of who 'we' are necessary in the first place. Different South Africans also have very different future possibilities from one another; if we are all post- anything, some of us are more post- than others, and many of us are differently post- from one another. Nevertheless, in the course of this book, I will use these terms because they are a convenient shorthand: I use post-colonial and post-apartheid mainly as historical markers, although post-colonial also refers to a body of work or an approach in the academy. Neo-colonial and neo-apartheid are used when I want to acknowledge that the inheritances of colonialism and apartheid are still with us, that these historical events have shaped the present in ways that make the moniker 'post-' optimistic. After all, the fact of this book, an engagement with Shakespeare in South Africa, is evidence of the neo-colonial reality in which we live as post-apartheid South Africans.

CHAPTER 1

Shakespeare in English, English in South Africa

In her 2007 European Union Literary Award-winning first novel, Kopana Matlwa presents an engaged critique of the primacy of English in the 'new' South Africa. *Coconut* is the story of two young women, Ofilwe and Fikile. The former is part of the emerging black middle class, and has 'lost' her culture for an Englished identity in a world of 'white' privilege that will never truly accept or know her. Eating with her family at an otherwise whites-only restaurant, she thinks,

> *We dare not eat with our naked fingertips, walk in generous groups, speak merrily in booming voices ... They will scold us if we dare, not with their lips ... because the laws prevent them from doing so, but with their eyes. They will shout, 'Stop acting black!'* [1]

The latter is desperate to acquire the glamour and power of whiteness in order to escape the poverty and deprivation she sees as intrinsically 'black':

> *'And you, Fikile, what do you want to be when you grow up?'*
> *'White, teacher Zola. I want to be white.'* ...

> *'But Fikile dea r... why would you want to do that ... ?'*
> *'Because it's better.'*
> *'What makes you think that, Fikile?'*
> *'Everything.'* [2]

Part of acquiring whiteness and the class advancement that goes with it is acquiring English, and with it an implictly Anglo-American culture which is relentlessly 'white'. This is Ofilwe's ironic ABC:

> *After-Sun. Bikini. Ballet. Barbie and Ken. Cruise. Disneyland. Disco. Diamonds and Pearls. Easter Egg. Fettucine. Frappe. Fork and Knife. Gymnastics. Horse Riding. Horticulture. House in the Hills. Indoor Cricket. Jungle Gym. Jacuzzi. Jumping Jacks and Flip Flacks. Khaki. Lock. Loiter. Looks like Trouble. Maid. Native. Nameless.*

> *No, not me, Madam. Napoleon. Ocean. Overthrow. Occupy and Rule. Palace. Quantity. Quantify. Queen of England. Red. Sunscreen. Suntan. Sex on the Beach. Tinkerbell. Unicorn. Oopsy daisy. Unwrap them all at once! Video Games. World Wide Web. Wireless Connection. Xmas. Yo-yo Diet. You, You and You. Zero guilt.* [3]

Matlwa's novel is an attack on ongoing systemic racism and its links to what the book sees as the power bloc that is whiteness and Englishness: the two are inseparable. Thinking of her cousins in the townships, whose parents did not advance economically and who did not have access to the education she was given, Ofilwe says:

*I spoke the TV language; the one Daddy spoke at work,
the one Mama never could get right, the one that spoke
of sweet success.*

*How can I possibly listen to those who try to convince
me otherwise? What has Sepedi ever done for them?
Look at those sorrowful cousins of mine who think that
a brick is a toy. Look at me. Even the old people know I
am special.... They smile at me and say, 'You, our child,
must save all your strength for your books.' Do you see,
I always tell my cousins, that they must not despair, as
soon as my schooling is over I will come back and teach
them English and then they will be special too?* [4]

Shakespeare has a small but significant cameo role in the book,
as the rhetorical trappings in the speech and subjectivity of an
emasculated, abusive, poor, black man with a useless English
education. Unlike Ofilwe's English, which makes her special,
Uncle's Shakespearean English just makes him exploitable and,
in Fikile's words, pathetic.

This book takes *Coconut*'s understanding of the intertwining
of whiteness, Englishness, and social and economic power as its
starting point and its end point. Apposite to this discussion is the
assumption embedded in the very idea of a coconut that culture
and identity are and should be contained, controlled, pure, and
raced. Immediately following the extract above, where Ofilwe
naïvely celebrates how her English, linked to her class status,
makes her 'special', Matlwa inserts the following vignette:

Katlego Matuana-George, dressed in a Vanguard
Creation, sells the cover of this month's *Fresh*
magazine. Katlego, the former principal dancer of

> the renowned Von Holt School of Modern Dancing ...
> shares that she tries to have as many equestrian
> weekends with her husband Tom at their farm in the
> north as possible. It helps to ground her and allows
> her the latitude to reflect on her life. [5]

'Katlego Matuana-George' is not a character in the book and does not recur. She is clearly a satire on a blackness saturated with class privilege and the veneer of whiteness that goes with it. Her clothes, her 'modern' dancing, her white husband and their ranch 'in the north' are all indicators of a blackness not just altered but ameliorated by its exposure to cultural colonisation.

The relationship between all these markers – identity, language, race, and, as Matlwa's novel also painfully shows through Fikile's association of personal advancement with whiteness, class – is exemplified in the history of how English came to South Africa, who spoke it, why, and how. Gender is also a factor in this history, not least because it is often missing. One of the many interesting contributions *Coconut* makes to this issue is the fact of its protagonists' and its author's gender – the first comment by a female insider since Noni Jabavu's autobiographical *The Ochre People* (1963). [6] Gendered experience features in aspects of the novel's detail – in Ofilwe's internalisation of 'yo-yo dieting', and in both girls' obsessions with their hair and Fikile's with her green contact lenses. It also features in the implication at the end of the novel that Fikile is headed towards sexual exploitation by an old white man: '*Anything worth having in life comes at a price, a price that is not always easy to pay. Maybe Paul is right ... He seems to really like me ... What do I have to lose?*' [7] The obvious answer, everything she has left of her already battered sense of self, speaks in a gendered way to what the novel presents as the cost of exposure to a world by now saturated with commodification, economic, social, and linguistic power relations, and perverted racialised values. As I explained in the introduction and as I will go on to explore in more detail in this chapter, while it is imperative to remain cognisant of the very real violent histories behind this understanding of identity, race, and language in the region, the either/or presentation of the possibilities for being South African in *Coconut* are limiting. More than this, the argument that to be black means one cannot also own English or modernity is reductive of current identifications and ignorant of an extremely rich and important local history as well.

Exploring the multilayered history of English in South Africa – as a language, as a formal field of study, in its relation to the processes and structures of colonialism – enables us to see some of the complexities of what it means to be South African: what it means now, and what it always has meant, despite rigorous attempts by apartheid engineering to suggest otherwise. [8] This social and political history, embedded as it is in multiple complicities and contradictions of identification, enables us to see why *Coconut*'s vision of the relationship between race, culture, privilege, and language, important as it is not least for its articulation of intransigent structural racism as well as for its introduction of gender as an important issue, is flawed. More than this, it can be dangerous. This is evident when we look at how the link between race, culture, language, and a sense that privilege is 'white' (disavowing the new economic privilege on the rise in the country) is being deployed when some politicians find their backs to the proverbial wall. Just one example is erstwhile ANC Youth League President Julius Malema's extraordinary verbal attack on BBC journalist Jonah Fisher in 2010. Fisher challenged Malema's criticism of Zimbabwe's opposition Movement for Democratic Change party for having offices in the affluent Johannesburg area of Sandton. This, Malema suggested, made them inauthentic.

Fisher pointed out that Malema himself lives in Sandton. Malema's response was to call for Fisher's removal from the press conference, accusing him of racism, and of participating in the white/English control of international media spaces which by definition disrespected the ANC and black people in general. [9] Malema's defensive aggression, here and elsewhere, is predicated on the presentation of white people as by definition not, and anti-, African, as conspiring to keep economic privilege to themselves, and as enacting a politics of resentment towards black men who have 'made it' in 'white' terms. In this racialised performance, there is no room for the idea that to be South African is to exist in a complex personal and social relation to markers of race, privilege, language, and culture.

I am not presuming to sum up the content of a South African identity, or to contain it in a label. Focussing on an aspect of how English and Englishness has helped to shape some of us, and has in turn been shaped in specific ways here, enables us to see that binary constructions of identity and culture are artificial constructs. It also enables us to see the ways in which some of the positions taken by our current leadership in the name of an African identity politics are much more historically complicated than their rhetorical performances might suggest. Whether this is Thabo Mbeki's investment in an African Renaissance, [10] Julius Malema's invocation of an old colonial rhetoric, often to silence opposition [11] (which I think of as Mugabism, in its patent self-servicing and when placed together with the self-enriching activities of these men who claim to act in the name of a post-colonial justice for 'the people'), or Jacob Zuma's deployment of tribal authenticity to justify his gender politics, [12] these constructions of the genuinely African rely on a binary version of whiteness. This politically useful Africanness, while it speaks to real, ongoing issues of inherited inequalities which remain primarily raced, is artifically purified, purged of the messiness of historical interaction. Examining the role of English in colonising South Africa, and the ongoing legacies which have resulted, is one way to point to the actual complexities at work, and to counter the current tendencies to return to a simplified and simplistic racialised discourse of us and them. It also forces us to keep centre stage the issue of class and gender privilege that has always been a part of this history, and, of course, to acknowledge the ways in which colonialism denigrated 'black' cultures.

I aim to investigate the complexities of Englishness in South Africa through the thoroughly overdetermined figure of Shakespeare – overdetermined simultaneously as the sign of English Literature and as the sign of universal humanity, and overdetermined as a marker of culture. We cannot, and should not, deny our fraught history of unequal power relations and colonial, apartheid, and, indeed, neo-colonial and neo-apartheid exploitations. Nevertheless, the presence of English here, as a language and as a series of texts available to South African writers, has always meant more than the simplistic presentation of 'the West's' cultural hegemony over a putatively 'pure' African space or subject can capture.

In this chapter I sketch what English first meant to those South African subjects who encountered it as formational of their social and, to a greater or lesser degree, personal identities. This takes us back to the time of the mission schools and the initial colonial encounters which helped to forge a new class of African men. Within the history of an English and Englishing education, I will focus on Shakespeare's role as the ubertext of English Literature, and the way 'his' texts and 'his' signifying potential were taken up by a specific, central figure. Solomon Plaatje, a founding member of the ANC and of indigenous journalism, and a political and linguistic activist, was also a founding South

African Shakespearean. His use of Shakespeare combines these two activisms, demonstrating how Shakespeare has been made indigenous. Crucially, Plaatje's life story and his work also demonstrate how the South African history of oppression and struggle were formative of this indigenous Shakespeare, which went on to exceed colonial control.

I suggest ways in which this colonial history, and Shakespeare's place in it in particular via the example of Plaatjie, [13] can be read as a complex, complicitous, contradictory commentary on why colonial binaries like the West/Africa, or English/indigenous languages, or Shakespeare/indigenous cultures do not adequately describe who we are. I am not saying that Shakespeare's universality made 'him' available to Plaatje or other South Africans. As should be clear by now, I am suspicious of the politics of universality. Neither am I suggesting that Shakespeare was a colonising force whose influence created coconuts in the original sense. Although Shakespeare can be said to be an agent of coconuttiness from the beginning, in that the texts and their symbolic weight influenced the writing styles and psyches of some South Africans from within an education system that affected their personal subjectivities, these first coconuts should be seen to stand for an aspect of our history we can value. I want to show how, as an instance of one kind of South Africanness, our history both reveals the immense and significant investments of all kinds in the construction of the figure of Shakespeare, and also demonstrates why we cannot simply dismiss 'him' as a Western, colonial import. But first: why Shakespeare? Why is Shakespeare the gold standard of English Literature and Literariness?

Shakespeare in/and English

English as a subject has its own disciplinary history. Within the field of study that is English Literature, or what I will often designate Eng Lit, Shakespeare occupies a special place because of 'his' canonicity. Why Shakespeare became 'Shakespeare' in this context, why it was this particular writer whose texts came to stand for all that Eng Lit is and should be, is an ongoing question whose answer very much depends on your ideological positioning for or against the idea of literature as transcendental and apolitical.

As part of its development as a discipline, English Literature was fundamentally concerned to find ways to identify and evaluate the highest, best expressions of what it means to be human. Whether the origins of the discipline are considered to be in the emergence of the humanities from the study of rhetoric and from the European culture wars of the eighteenth century, in Matthew Arnold's nineteenth-century educational interventions, in colonial education practices, or in the professionalisation of the subject in the early twentieth century, Eng Lit has been developed around a concern to identify and evaluate 'the best' written cultural expressions of human life, even if those criteria have since been radically expanded. [14]

However, as a number of critics have pointed out, the project of developing a canon of the best literature in English was always implicated in a complex political field that it disavowed for a long time. For example, a collection of essays edited by Peter Widdowson sketched the discipline's various ideological and material constituting factors; Gauri Viswanathan has detailed the colonial politics behind the development of the formal study of Eng Lit; Terry Eagleton has argued that its institutionalisation was informed by a nostalgic, conservative ideological programme, and one deeply implicated in class and gender politics. More recently, Neil Rhodes has also argued for the imbrications of gender and class politics in the development of English Studies, from as far back as the Renaissance. [15]

In Shakespeare Studies in particular, the universal Shakespeare which is one of the cornerstones of the discipline came under fire for being classed, raced, and gendered. Furthermore, 'his' supposed apolitical universality was revealed to be ideologically complicit with the oppressive bourgeois practices of the state. [16] Shakespeare's putative universality was interrogated in material terms, and responsible historical accounts attempted to trace the process through which 'his' reputation was accrued, instead of assuming its self-perpetuating and self-evident nature. [17] It is these investigations which have made possible the challenge to the universal Shakespeare as self-evidently the best human culture has to offer, when that apparently universal human culture happens to belong to a specific time and place and does not, in fact, speak equally or equally easily to all humans.

Despite these academic 'discoveries', Shakespeare retains 'his' place in popular culture as the marker of high human culture. [18] In a South African context, this positionality has been used to invoke a range of references, resonances, and self-fashionings, as the rest of this book illustrates. For now, the point I wish to stress is that despite a history which clearly demonstrates a vexed, complex, ambivalent, contradictory position for Shakespeare in our region, and from there for the Englishness 'he' has come to stand for, Shakespeare keeps coming up as a signifier of a binary relation. This relation is more or less overtly raced and classed, depending on the situation.

That Shakespeare keeps standing for something else – culture, whiteness, literature (implicitly English) – is clear in the commotion which followed a group of teachers' suggestion to the Gauteng Education Department in 2001 that certain Shakespeare plays be banned from school syllabi. Plays earmarked for removal included *Anthony and Cleopatra* and *Othello* (for being racist), *Julius Caesar* ('because it elevates men'), and *King Lear* (for being 'full of violence and despair'). [19] These teachers were clearly motivated by some sort of awareness of the findings of the work outlined above, and trying to be responsible about the ideological power of Shakespeare and the messages being transmitted through education. But both the attack on the Shakespearean texts, and the responses in the press, spoke to a host of other anxieties underlying what this literature stood for in people's minds. [20] This is not to deny that any discussion of the details, role, or purpose of English literary studies in post-apartheid South Africa must take cognisance of the debates about Shakespeare as an agent of various kinds of colonisation, as well as the debates about colonising languages in neo-colonial situations. [21] Shakespeare, as the icon of Eng Lit and of a particular kind of cultured Englishness, remains a potent signifier of what English stands for in South Africa, even if what exactly that is, is variable depending on the times and the person or community.

English in South Africa

If there is a lingua franca in South Africa, it is Zulu. [22] But English is the language of power – the means to social and economic advancement – as it was in the days of the mission schools. From the early 1840s, missionaries facilitated the first printed vernacular texts. These were all religious. However, South Africans wrote Christian texts not only because they were converts: as colonisation impacted on the existing social, political, and economic structures, Christianity and an education in English and the Englishness it transmitted were the means to succeed in the new system. [23] In post-apartheid South Africa, English remains the language it is necessary to know in order to advance economically and politically, and so socially. [24]

Despite never having been the most-spoken language, in other words, English was the most powerful language during the development of formal education in the region, and the social changes this system helped to effect. Leon de Kock points to the inescapable multiple violences of this history when he says:

> [T]he orthodoxy of English as a dominant medium of educational discourse in South Africa, and the institutionalisation of this discourse (by which English 'literature' is privileged as an area of study), was won by blood ... the ascendancy of English as a principal medium for social empowerment among many black South Africans was secured in the nineteenth century on frontier battlefields by colonial soldiers. [25]

The supremacy of English within the educated elite carried through into the formation of the liberation movement, whose leaders were from this elite. With the passing of the Bantu Education Act in 1953 as part of the formalisation of apartheid, the mission schools were effectively closed during the 1950s. The Bantu Education Act was designed to terminate access to the social and economic mobility enabled by a mission-school education because of the threat this educated class fraction posed, as a source of leadership, and to the increasingly white-protectionist labour market. It is from this fraction that the ANC was born, and thus from which the upper echelons of the current political ruling class in South Africa have emerged, at least until the presidency of Jacob Zuma (this change is significant for my final conclusions about the symbolic status Shakespeare now occupies in the South African public sphere).

English was not only a tool of self- as well as social empowerment under colonialism. It was also useful during apartheid. Es'kia Mphahlele, one of our finest writers in English from the mission-educated generations, has written about the ways in which English functioned as a language of resistance during apartheid. [26] He also spoke about the personal gains brought by a fluency in English as the language and the culture that helped to shape the boys who attended the mission schools: 'English which was not our mother tongue, gave us power, power to master the external world which came to us through it.' [27] If English has always been a language of personal power as well as an aspirational language, its status as such was exacerbated by apartheid policies of 'retribalisation' and by Bantu Education, which made it clear that education in the venacular was intended to be second-rate. [28]

Another reason English enjoyed its status as the language of resistance under apartheid was the (now problematised) position of Afrikaans as the language of the oppressor. As the language of the educated, English is implicated in class hierarchies which are more important now than they were under apartheid, when the exigencies of Struggle called for the sublimation of differences among the oppressed. In post-apartheid South Africa, as Graham Pechey points out, '[f]luency in English is virtually synonymous with literacy', [29] which means with class advantage. *Coconut* ends up despairing of this fact, as it concludes with the words of a clearly good man whom Fikile meets on the train, and who talks about watching his daughter on the playground at her elite school. At first he acknowledges the integration that an education in English has enabled:

> And then suddenly a little chocolate girl walks past me, hand in hand with the cutest half-metre milk bar I have ever seen in my life. Both of them are chatting away ... He smiles at the memory. Wow! I thought, look how happy they are.

But then he goes on:

> They were so joyful, those kids. But, you know, I couldn't shake the feeling that they were only happy because they didn't know. Don't get me wrong, the school is remarkable, it really is ... [J]ust by looking at Palesa, you can just see that she is such an inspired little girl with so much to offer the world. Compared to other children her age in the township, who go to black schools, she is miles ahead ... But, I can't shake a certain feeling ... [L]istening to all those little black faces yelping away in English ... just broke my heart ... Standing at the edge of that playground, I watched little spots of amber and auburn become less of what Africa dreamed of and more of what Europe thought we ought to be. [30]

Palesa's father could be describing a child at a colonial mission school when he speaks of the 'opportunities those children get at that school', [31] and the way her education positions her as someone with 'so much to offer the world', specifically because it equips her with a fluency in English and an acculturation to the dominant ideological system. Of course, notable again is that the coconuts in this book are all female, with the exception of the failed coconut, Fikile's uncle. This is one change which marks progress of a sort from then till now: opportunities are available to some girls as well as to their brothers. However, Matlwa is emphasising not the opportunity, but the cost of coconuttiness, in part by sliding back into the reified, binary positions exemplified by 'Africa' and 'Europe' in the mind of Palesa's dad.

Scholars from a range of disciplines have examined the implications for elite South Africans of the hegemonic dominance of English. The mission school disseminated what Graham Duncan has called 'coercive agency': [32] along with Christianity, the missions taught a colonial and colonising ideology which shaped their students even as the black South African men resisted and responded to the message that their cultures and languages were in need of improvement and replacement. Scholars of mission schools and their effects, and the early South African writers in English, all emphasise the 'ambiguous qualification' [33] which an education in English language and literary culture entailed. For example, in his autobiography *Tell Freedom*, Peter Abrahams, one of the first black South African writers to acquire an international career and the first to write an autobiography in English, details the effects of his mission-school education in pre-apartheid days. It gave him his vocation (specifically, he says, Shakespeare inspired in him the desire to write, and to become educated in English literature). It gave him a deep sense of justice and of a shared humanity through the Christian ideology he was taught. It also made the hypocrisies of South Africa in the world outside the schoolroom walls inescapably obvious and intolerable. And, as he goes on to chart in his life story, his education makes it impossible for him to return to his family and the community from which he came. [34]

As Abrahams suggests, the Englished South African subject has been described as split. While a postmodern understanding would see all subjectivity as split or fractured, and would understand this as unproblematic, the splitting effects of English have been repeatedly presented as fracturing a subject who would otherwise be authentically whole: in saving, English also spoils. Bloke Modisane writes bitterly of the experience of being a 'Situation', 'the eternal alien between two worlds' [35] as a result of his propensity for a cultured 'white society', membership of which was denied him by early apartheid legislation and attitudes. Duncan traces this split condition back to the mission schools, describing how Lovedale created 'dislocated individuals and groups', alienated from their societies of birth and also excluded from 'the Western European lifestyle they aspired to'. [36] But the Englished South African's 'Situation' can be read as something other than the position of eternal exclusion, particularly if one is looking pre- and post-apartheid.

English has always played a more complex role in South African identities and societies than Ngugi wa Thiong'o's famous explication allows. I do not wish to deny the region's painful history of struggle, to celebrate its effects, or to blithely overlook the reality of ongoing relations of material and discursive power kept in place by the dominance of English resulting from this history. However, colonised subjects made use of colonial tools of oppression, often in order to construct themselves as resisting subjects, albeit with complications and complicities. This use implies a process that resulted not only in the cultural colonisation of the African mind, but also in African ownership of colonial texts, icons, and languages. It is a contradictory and traumatic process, with ramifications for identity on personal and cultural levels. But language can become a tool for the comprador speaker, because comprador identity, the access to the colonial world gained though language use, comes about not solely through the acquisition of the colonial language, but 'through the act of speaking itself, the act of self-assertion involved in using the language of the colonizer'. [37] The subject speaking English in South Africa will always be more than the sum of the colonial process; the forms taken by agency cannot be underestimated. [38] If millions of Africans by now speak English, is English not an African language, one as deeply implicated in history as any other language – not universal, in other words, and not straightforwardly liberating, but 'authentically', contradictorily African? Like any other aspect of identity? Like the African coconut?

Solomon Plaatje: The first South African coconut

For elite African men at the turn of the century of high colonialism, English was a very important medium as well as a personal and artistic source of useful and sometimes enriching content. It was, as it remains, a means for socio-economic advancement. It was a mine of literary wealth, interesting for its own sake and for the messages about universal humanity conveyed through the teaching of Eng Lit. Deploying English and the literature that went with it was the means to publicly stake a claim to personhood in the terms of the ruling regime; it enabled a demonstration and provided a vocabulary that was meant to help in the fight against colonial patronage and its hardening racism. Leon de Kock has shown how and why African intellectuals seeking to forge a literary and human presence embraced English as a 'universal' and universalising language. He notes also the complexities and complicities of this position:

The writing of 'literature' in English was an uneasy negotiation: in its dense web of textuality were multiple constraints and restraints. One didn't just take English and make literature in a vacuum ... Many early works of black South African writing in English attest to this unease in the very forms, idioms, and registers employed in writing for a readership that did not really exist in any significant numbers except as an imaginary community where English and the values it was held to represent approximated the ideals of civil egalitarianism ... English was a discursive site riven with contradiction – offering entry to a larger world, a more global imaginary, but hedged by the constraints of a colonizing ideology. [39]

De Kock goes on to offer an argument for recognising the complexity of African identifications with British identity and Western acculturation, for taking seriously the desire to participate in and to own what these things offered and stood for: civility, modernity, Christian brotherhood, equality. He argues that the South African response to colonisation was never one of pure oppositionality; instead, African leaders used the discourses, ideas, and ideologies brought by the colonisers to demand inclusion into the civil imaginary and into state structures, and sought to counter racism by calling for the recognition of their ability to live up to all the terms designated by the colonisers as the marks of human development and 'civilisation'.

Equally, Bhekizizwe Peterson has recently stressed how writing in English by African intelligentsia at the turn of the twentieth century was an act of self-assertion, a performance of African modernity: 'The new African intelligentsia drew on their mastery of literacy and African orature in order to claim and defend their rights as modern citizens.' [40] They engaged with British imperialism in the terms in which it presented itself to them: as a viable ally against Afrikaner nationalism. Nonetheless, they occupied a vexed position. As loyal citizens of Britain, they articulated a commitment to, and in so doing called upon, the liberal values being asserted in the name of Empire. At the same time they faced ongoing and worsening hardship as the hypocrisy of British liberal discourse regarding race in South Africa became increasingly clear. English became at once a resource in the fight for political rights and for the rights of indigenous cultures, a creolising force in personal identities and in cultural developments, a marker of acculturation and modernisation, a false promise ... complex and contradictory indeed. [41]

We could reformulate these nuanced descriptions of the complexities of identification and performances at the time, as signifiers of a reformulated coconuttiness. This new definition reclaims the pejorative term as signifying a form of elite African modernity that is as much a 'true' part of African history, and Struggle history, as any other. We see all the markers of this coconuttiness in the work of Solomon Plaatje, and the double-edgedness of it in the progression of his life's writing as it responded to the events he lived through.

Plaatje's life story is by now well known; I will not rehearse it in detail here. [42] Born in 1876, he was a man of extraordinary ability and range of activity. He was a founding member of the political organisation that would become the ANC, a leading journalist, a diarist and letterist, a linguist, a professional interpreter (he spoke nine languages), a 'native' ethnographer deeply rooted in his Barolong identity, a Christian, the first black South African novelist in English, and the first translator of Shakespeare in southern Africa. He also wrote political texts which are literary in their skill, and travelled internationally campaigning for the increasingly receding rights of black South Africans as the twentieth century began. He was largely self-educated and life-educated, coming of age in the cosmopolitan town of Kimberley, [43] but he did have connections to the mission-school system. He grew up and was partially educated, until 1894, at the mission station at Pniel. He died in 1932, still fighting for the dwindling political and linguistic rights of black South Africans.

In terms of my argument, Plaatje is the archetypal coconut for a number of reasons. He was '[a]rguably the pre-eminent literary figure present at the moment of the first formation of South Africa as a single political entity'. [44] This literary skill was manifest in both English and Setswana, and in his complex creations and translations between the two cultures, their literatures, and the forms those literatures took.

Indeed, Plaatje has been read as the first, and the most proficient, African writer in the acts of translation in all senses: 'Plaatje was … *literally*, almost *quintessentially*, interdiscursive.' This interdiscursivity includes the ways in which he incorporated orature into his writing, allowing African practices and values to interpenetrate with the English in which he was also highly skilled. [45] As a result he created what is arguably a truly South African literary discourse, made up of both/and, not either/or. For example, Deborah Seddon has written about Plaatje's interdiscursive mediation between Setswana orality and Shakespeare, arguing that he 'reactivates' the oral elements in Shakespeare. [46] This is one way to recognise Plaatje's contribution to Shakespeare, without privileging Shakespeare as the signifier of a culture and a process of acculturation to which Plaatje was subjected. Instead, in Seddon's reading, Shakespeare is equally subjected to Plaatje. This reading recognises Plaatje's agency and creativity.

Plaatje was interdiscursive in other, non-literary ways as well. As a global traveller in political campaigns, Plaatje was part of the multinational group of colonial elites who influenced one another's nationalist identities and agendas. [47] While this international colonial resistance has been shown by Boehmer to characterise and influence the development of profoundly national anti-colonial struggles, it foreshadows modern globalised formations. As much as he was a man of his times, Plaatje was also a coconut for being 'a forerunner, a harbinger of the ... transnational networking which ... has distinguished late twentieth-century South African culture in particular'. [48]

There are other ways in which Plaatje's coconuttiness presaged some of our current issues. Boehmer maps the complexities of Plaatje's identifications – as a spokesman for 'his people' and a member of the petit-bourgeois educated elite, as a loyal subject of Britain and of the Empire, as a self-consciously 'civilised' black man, and as a tireless critic and skilled satirist of the hypocrisies and limitations of his white rulers. [49] Boehmer characterises Plaatje's multifaceted, paradoxical self-positioning as 'that overdetermined Janus ability to face in at least two if not several directions at once'. [50] His multilingualism, as much as his role as cultural and linguistic translator in the permanent contact zone that was his life and milieu, made him emblematic of a South African possible way of being – always bearing in mind the class, if no longer gender, elitism of this position, its reliance on educational opportunities and the social flexibility they bring. Boehmer also suggests that in his writing style he instantiated the racial inseparability for which he so fervently campaigned all his working life. [51]

Finally, Plaatje is a coconut because of his association with Shakespeare, that ultimate signifier of fluency in English and of Englishness. He has been appreciated as a potential South

African Shakespeare. [52] He has also been seen as a representative of the emerging petit-bourgeois African class whose love of Shakespeare becomes a delineating marker of education and civility, and he has been both praised and criticised accordingly. [53]

Plaatje and Shakespeare

Plaatje makes multiple and repeated use of Shakespeare across his oeuvre of political and creative writing, as well as in his linguistic activism. For example, his novel *Mhudi* (first published in 1930), which was in part an engagement with the increasingly oppressive legal situation in general, and land politics in particular, draws on Shakespeare thematically and stylistically. [54] He also quotes King Lear in *Native Life in South Africa* in order to authorise his rage and despair at the effects of the 1913 Land Act. [55] Furthermore, in his introduction to *Diphosophoso*, his Setswana translation of *A Comedy of Errors*, Plaatje says that he translates Shakespeare in order to prove Setswana's worth and thus attempt to ensure its survival; he is clearly invoking Shakespeare's status as the best English can do to demand equal respect for a language fast being transformed by colonial and missionary intervention.

To illustrate the creativity of coconuttiness as well as its multiple simultaneous positionalities, I use as an example here what Plaatje does with and to Shakespeare in his contribution to Isaac Gollancz's *A Book of Homage to Shakespeare* (1916). Gollancz's edited text, assembled for the 1916 tercentenary celebrations of Shakespeare's life, was an extraordinary work of colonial writing. Coppelia Kahn has shown how, as it drew together contributions from within and across the Empire in the name of Shakespeare as the signifier of English and Englishness itself, the collection allowed for the cultural performance of an idealised, reified Englishness *and* a counter-performance from national Others which undermined this project: 'The poet of Englishness, readily available to any imperial subject educated in "the English-speaking tradition", is blithely enlisted in support of agendas to unseat that very tradition.' [56] This is done by activating the paradoxical meaning of Shakespeare as at once quintessentially English and the embodiment of human universality. This ideological project – to make Englishness at once specific and universal – is part of the core work of Empire, Khan suggests. She shows how the presence of imperial voices in the *Book of Homage* was enlisted to confirm the universality of Shakespeare and thus of Englishness, and, in the logic of the universal Bard, of Englishness and thus of Shakespeare. But she also shows how the colonies had other ideas, as the colonies always do. She discusses the ways a number of contributers, Plaatje among them, make use of Shakespeare's signification to assert their own political points, thus ensuring they 're-envision Shakespeare, dismantling his links to England and to empire'. [57]

Kahn focuses on Plaatje's linguistic activism for Setswana, arguing that here, as I have suggested above he did elsewhere, 'Plaatje respectfully engages Shakespeare in the project of preserving and/or reinventing his *own* culture'. [58] Kahn discusses the way Plaatje claims Shakespeare's texts for African cultural expressions,

> the forms customary and useful in Setswana culture ... Thus his tribute to Shakespeare serves not 'the English speaking tradition', but rather his own tradition, placed in danger of extinction precisely because of British imperialism, which at the same time provides Plaatje with some of the implements for its tenuous preservation. [59]

An example of this double-edged Shakespeare can be found in Plaatje's insistence that the deaths of 'King Edward VII and two great Bechuana Chiefs – Sebele and Bathoeng' could be equally marked by a quotation from Shakespeare. [60] Equally, his concluding sentence to his contribution to the *Book of Homage* stresses 'that some of the stories on which [Shakespeare's] dramas are based find equivalents in African folk-lore'. [61] This is the best illustration, under the circumstances, of the universal quality of African culture, and hence evidence that it is not Other, inferior, barbaric, or in need of alteration.

Seddon argues that we need to 'extend' this focus on how Plaatje used Shakespeare, to look in more detail at how he interdiscursively navigated his native orality, and the acts of translation in which he was engaged as a cultural and political activist. By circulating and performing orality in print, making use of the creative and political potentials in Shakespeare's texts in multiple ways, 'Plaatje's work sought to create and circulate alternative combinations of tradition and modernity within his own political and cultural context'. [62] Thus Plaatje can be read not only as invoking Shakespeare's status in the *Book of Homage* to counter racism and to make a claim for the equal humanity of Africans. His invocation of Shakespeare in this collection also functions to construct what I am calling a coconut consciousness, in the name of demonstrating the full complexity of what it meant to be an African, and an African subject of Empire.

David Schalkwyk comments on the complexities of Plaatje's modes of address to his different audiences, and how this is reflected in his use of pronouns. [63] Here is an example from the *Book of Homage*, where Plaatje compares Shakespeare's plays to the racist messages conveyed in contemporary films, one of them made by the Ku Klux Klan:

Shakespeare's dramas, on the other hand, show that nobility and valor, like depravity and cowardice, are not the monopoly of any color. Shakespeare lived over 300 years ago, but he appears to have had a keen grasp of human character. His description of things seems so inwardly correct that (in spite of our rapid means of communication and facilities for traveling) we of the present age have not yet equaled his acumen. [64]

Plaatje, writing in London, speaks to an English audience when he denotes himself and his audience as 'we of the present age'. In speaking in English, of Shakespeare, Plaatje demonstrates that he shares with his audience an appreciation of Shakespeare as well as a modern cosmopolitanism. Plaatje has claimed the language and its most famous son as his own, and in living that identity, in the act of writing, he self-consciously also counters typical colonial charges against African subjects of Empire, of barbarism or backwardness. At the same time, Plaatje's allusion to the inwardly *in*correct nature of 'the present age', 'in spite of our rapid means of communication and ... traveling', allows him to critique the ignorance implicit in the racism in the films to which he refers. He also implicitly invokes Shakespeare's putative universally human status to endorse this judgement.

In all this, we see how Plaatje used Shakespeare to make a claim for his, and his people's, already-proven inclusion in the realm of imperial citizenry and the modernity it claimed to stand for. This claim is indeed Janus-faced: in claiming space in imperial universality, Plaatje simultaneously deployed Shakespeare as 'a useful instrument with which to sustain his own culture, language, and political identity'. [65]

But Plaatje does not just have Shakespeare to use as a tool. Plaatje relates an anecdote of how Shakespeare's English functioned as the language of love between himself and his wife-to-be (they both read *Romeo and Juliet*, he goes on to say, since their cultural situation mimicked the play's):

> While reading *Cymbeline*, I met the girl who afterwards became my wife. I was not then as well acquainted with her language – the Xhosa – as I am now; and although she had a better grip of mine – the Sechuana – I was doubtful whether I could make her understand my innermost feelings in it, so in coming to an understanding we both used the language of educated people – the language which Shakespeare wrote – which happened to be the only official language of our country at the time. [66]

If this is allowed to be not just the chance for him to make a political point about English rule and the responsibilities that should implictly come with that status towards such obviously Anglo-identified subjects, but also the record of a moment of intimacy and connection not only through but with a literary text, Shakespeare is clearly not just a tool. 'His' texts, their literary power, their putatively universal messages have been interpolated and owned, claimed.

Plaatje and the others that followed him were Englished subjects, subjects of and in English. But not in a slavish or solely colonised sense, *pace* Ngugi wa Thiong'o's formulation. Reading Plaatje positively as a coconut is a way to take seriously the elite colonial subjectivity he can be made to represent. His paradoxical stance becomes the picture not of the ventriloquising subaltern, able only to mimic, however subversively. Taking Plaatje's coconuttiness seriously is a way to see him and the men of his class as far more complex than simply positioned in relation to the colonisers who may have had a lot to do with determining the terms of possibility for them, but certainly did not control their responses, much as they may have tried. Plaatje, and the coconuts who follow, born into the cultural, political, and social 'Situation' which was and is South Africa following on from Plaatje's time, were legitimate African subjects.

Indeed, Plaatje's coconuttiness could be said to exemplify the way identity functions, especially in as complex a space as post-apartheid South Africa:

> A subjectivity such as his, inhabiting a place of difference so clearly constructed for it and aspiring in every way to counter the fixed conceptions attached to it, can only be aware of the provisional nature of identity, especially as it is developed within cross-cultural representations. [67]

The spaces of human interaction after colonial contact, fraught and unequal as they were and as they remain, produced subjects who can never return to a place of imagined pure Africanness, if indeed such a place ever truly existed. Instead, for those of us able to occupy the elite space of even relative economic stability, coconuttiness can be the marker of a constituting interdiscursivity which is as African as the history of South Africa itself. Like Plaatje's Shakespeare, the African coconut is both/and, both Englished and transforming of Englishness. And this is a legitimate South African identity.

English in South Africa, Shakespeare in South Africa

There is no intrinsic reason why Shakespeare's texts should be made to speak to South African issues outside of the inheritances of the colonial system which entrenched Shakespeare as the paragon of literature. At the same time, there is an African Shakespearean tradition which exists in our history, which begins with Plaatje, and which is absent from most South Africans' experiences of what Shakespeare can and does mean. This is clear in Matlwa's novel, where the weak and emasculated Uncle stands for what the educated Englished black man can become in post-apartheid South Africa. This is a sharp comment on the figure of the earlier, mission-educated young man, who was meant to be groomed as a leader of 'his people', and was skilled to navigate the new system on their behalf:

> Uncle just came home after his first semester at the University of Cape Town with a letter of exclusion from the medical school in his bookbag ... He lay in bed for weeks sobbing ... and that was the end of Uncle the smart one, the one who spoke the white man's language, the one who would save us. [68]

For Matlwa, an educated woman writing in English about the benefits and costs of being an Englished African subject today, the figure of a constructed leader of 'his people' spouting Shakespeare is an aspirant doomed to fail in a corrupt and hypocritical system. This post-apartheid critique echoes the kinds of criticisms levelled against the men of Plaatje's ilk by a later generation of angry youth less willing to play the civil game in the face of politics in twentieth-century South Africa. [69] As I go on to argue in the last chapter, which looks in more detail at

Coconut, self-delusional Uncle might be what the Shakespearised coconut has become in post-apartheid South Africa. If, for Plaatje, Shakespeare was the embodiment of what Engish had to offer, in our times Shakespeare may be the embodiment of its empty promises. Given this move towards binary meanings, it remains important to remember that the subject of English – the language, the literature, and the figure of the South African made by and in English(ed) systems of power – becomes evidence for the actual complexity of the apparently oppositional positions English is increasingly invoked to endorse in the current political climate.

The history of Shakespeare in South Africa encapsulates the complex regional history of complicities, contestations, reclamations, and resistances which comprise the true meaning of the coconut. Material privilege, aspiration, identity politics, and race politics all adhere in messy and complicated ways to 'English' and to 'Shakespeare', as indeed they always have.

The chapters that follow demonstrate this complex, contradictory subject by offering case studies of what Shakespeare has been to, and for, a range of South African subject positions. It becomes clear how often 'he' is invoked to shore up an identity binary which draws its power from the privilege which (still) accrues to English and to the whiteness with which it is associated. This is one of Matlwa's points in *Coconut*. At the same time, as I have been arguing, the presence of a genuinely South African ownership of Shakespeare – complex, complicit, contradictory as this is – as seen in the work of Plaatje, for example, demonstrates the artificiality of this binary, and exposes discourses of African authenticity as artificial and impossibly nostalgic. It demonstrates the true melange which is by now a paradoxically 'authentic' South Africanness. That Shakespeare tends not to be invoked in this context in South Africa is a lesson not only in the politics of exclusion and social and personal power plays in the region. It is also evidence of what it is that still animates the symbolic power of 'Shakespeare' and the history of overpowering to which that symbol of English belongs.

CHAPTER 2

'Through Shakespeare's Africa':
'Terror and murder'?

In South Africa, the desire to make connections between Shakespeare's time and a contemporary local reality has a history that goes back to, at least, the work of Solomon Plaatje in the early twentieth century. The apparent parallels between the conditions of life in South Africa and Elizabethan England generated comment also in the 1950s, the 1980s, and post-apartheid in the 1990s. This chapter will discuss some of the different motivations for, and effects of, making a connection between South Africa and Shakespeare's England.

There are at least two ways in which such a comparison functions. On the one hand, as Plaatje's oeuvre demonstrates, and as the writing of the *Drum* staffers discussed below indicates, pointing to a connection between Shakespeare and Africanness can authorise the human and political 'relevance' and worth of African experience. On the other hand, as the reference later in this chapter to Antony Sher and Gregory Doran's production of *Titus Andronicus* in post-apartheid South Africa seeks to point out, the need to find connections between the two times and places can indicate a problematic understanding of relevance, the ideological implications of which belie the attempt at recognition encoded in the act of comparison. [1]

The question of relevance encodes specific strategies of identification that reveal the workings of cultural politics, and not of a literary universality. Shakespeare is not uniquely 'relevant' to South Africa because 'his' works offer us life lessons we cannot do without, or cannot access in other ways. As explored in chapter 1, Shakespeare is 'relevant' because of the role 'he' has played in the development of writing in English in the region, and the links between this cultural history and the political and psychic histories of South Africa. As such, Shakespeare has a meaning and a presence here that exceeds, even as it arises out of, colonial constructions of cultural worth. Shakespeare is also 'relevant' to South Africa because all culture belongs to everyone. Nevertheless, we need to continue to be cognisant of the politics of the desire for Shakespearean relevance. As I will argue in this chapter, making connections between Shakespeare and South Africa can function in a range of ways.

If Shakespeare informs what it means to be a coconut through what 'he' stands for as an icon of Englishness, of universal culture, of privilege, then 'his' value as an authorising force and a figure of identification can be as fraught as the identity of the coconut itself. Given – or in spite of – 'his' fraught history, how important is Shakespeare to the 'new' South Africa, and hence to our emerging cultural formations? Matlwa's novel suggests 'he' is worthless, that the mission-school history from which 'he' emerged has taken us to a place of post-apartheid cultural dispossession. *Coconut*'s coconuts are deprived and cheated by what Shakespeare stands for, not enriched by it. But Shakespeare's coconuttiness has a more complex applicability. The racial and class politics of this applicability pull in different directions depending on the moment in South African history when they are activated, and by whom.

'Watching an Elizabethan play': *Drum*'s Shakespeare

Englishman Anthony Sampson was editor of the famous *Drum* magazine, which, in the 1950s, developed into a forum for expressing the experiences and constructing the identities of men and women living in the urban slum community of Sophiatown in Johannesburg. [2] In the process, *Drum* established the careers of a group of writers who developed the short story and the autobiography as key South African genres, before and during the time that most of them went into exile following amendments to the 1950 Suppression of Communism Act. Sampson made numerous comparisons between Elizabethan England and the ghettos of Johannesburg, in order to explain the quality of the lifestyles he saw there. This analogy was taken up by some of the *Drum* writers: in passing, by Lewis Nkosi; in an article, by Can Themba; and in extended form in his autobiography, by Bloke Modisane. [3]

Sampson's analogy was different in kind to those made by his staff members. The latter's mobilisations illustrate the potential in the analogy for resistance against racist policies, which deny the humanity of those they seek to subjugate. Like Plaatje's strategic use of Shakespeare's signifying potential, the *Drum* writers also rely on the fact that if apparently less civilised Africans can deploy the exemplar of English culture, and can point to similarities between what it meant to be African and the time that produced Shakespeare, then the connection is proof of the worth of the denigrated African experience of, or approach to, life.

Oxford-educated Sampson had a degree in Elizabethan drama. He overlaid his understanding of the conditions of Shakespeare's time onto what he saw happening in Sophiatown. This enabled him to enjoy and romanticise ghetto life in early apartheid South Africa: '[A]ll that frenzied activity... seemed to me to be every bit a Shakespearean play with terror and murder waiting in the wings.' [4] 'It was wildly romantic.' [5] In his autobiography, he wrote:

> It came to me suddenly that I was watching an Elizabethan play. It was as if the characters had tripped straight from the stage of the Globe, lugging their dead bodies with them. Sophiatown had all the exuberant youth of Shakespeare's London. It was the same upstart slum, with people coming from a primitive country life to the tawdry sophistication of the city's fringes. Death and the police state were round the corner: and there was the imminent stage direction: Exeunt with bodies. [6]

It is true that the responses of those who lived under the increasingly difficult conditions of the times – gangsters, good-time girls, shebeen queens (brewers and sellers of liquor, usually from their homes, at a time when it was illegal for black people to drink alcohol), and more conventional workers – were inventive, colourful, innovative, and energetic. Sophiatown was also a violent, hectic, squalid place, 'surrounded by a surface of uncertainty and hostility, epitomized by the threat of removal which hung over it from 1939 ... a huge generosity of spirit co-existed with conditions that made it a "deplorable, sickening slum"'. [7]

To understand this culturally hybrid, politically oppressive, and socially dangerous milieu in terms of Elizabethan England is at once to validate it and to establish a metaphor that, in its continual application to African life in South Africa, also serves to construct African life as premodern, chaotic, and, by definition, violent in a glorious way. In a South African context, given the terms of a colonial history that constructed Africans as, at best, children to the West's adulthood and, at worst, savages to its civilisation, this analogy too often reinscribes a construction of Africanness that underlies some of the justifications of the colonial system. [8] The putatively shared violence of Elizabethan England and of 'Africa' is taken up by some of the *Drum* staffers, and by Sher and Doran in their justifications for staging *Titus*. The different meanings generated signify the differing potentialities in what Shakespeare can stand for. It becomes clear that the position of the coconut is not singular. As much as it can be complicit with the kind of race politics exemplified by Sher and Doran's use of Shakespeare and the idea of 'Africa' they assume, it is equally the provenance of important South African writers such as Sol Plaatje and Can Themba.

Shakespeare's 'fraternal hand': Can Themba

Shakespeare – as an embodiment of literary education and linguistic aptitude, and as a moral exemplar – was part of a discourse of resistance in the writing of, and about, *Drum* magazine at the time when apartheid was being formalised. Can Themba co-opted a range of Shakespeare's plays in order to offer a complexly ironic critique of apartheid South Africa in 'Through Shakespeare's Africa', an article published in *The New African* in 1963. [9] This article is akin to Wole Soyinka's use of *Antony and Cleopatra* [10] in its ironic density and complicated rhetorical manoeuvres. In addition to offering a series of political and cultural critiques (which demonstrate the specific relation between the two realms in apartheid South Africa), Themba presents himself, through his use of Shakespeare, as a kind of coconut, a performance of self-fashioning which is an assertion of worth in the face of apartheid's construction of the tribal 'native', and also a highly gendered act of revenge.

Themba starts by asserting that violence is endemic to Africa in a way it is not to other places, such as 'Chicago ... Rome or Venice'. [11] It is no coincidence that Themba singles out America and familiar locations from Shakespeare's plays (he will go on to talk in most detail about *Julius Caesar* and *Othello*). As I will illustrate shortly, he combines the two dominant discourses most available to him as a product of Sophiatown to demonstrate his position within modernity: Americanisation, and Shakespeare.

African violence, like, implicitly, the vibrant and glorious Shakespearean violence characterised by Sampson (Themba begins his article with a reference to Sampson's analogy), is not just 'brutality'. That would be 'a kind of bore', and would not capture 'the arresting high drama of life'. Themba is engaging here with the familiar constructions of African chaos and barbarism, 'the excesses of adventure writers and narrators of jungle-life stories'. African violence is not the violence of the jungle, not the unthinking actions of animals, but the human violence of Shakespearean emotions and intrigues: 'the action, the passion, the lasciviousness, the high drama'. The excesses of African life are the dramatic excesses of the plays which represent the best and most human of world culture: 'This, Shakespeare would have understood without the interpolations of the scholars, and in this wise the world of Shakespeare reaches out a fraternal hand to the throbbing heart of Africa.' [12] Far from being less than human, Africans are the embodiment of what it means to be human.

Shakespeare's 'fraternal hand', as constructed by Themba, allows for much more than one moment of recognition, which works by allowing the Shakespearean to be the node of translation that explains and authorises 'the throbbing heart of Africa'. With an irony characteristic of many of the *Drum* writers' strategies of emotional containment, Themba goes on to use the relationship he has constructed between Shakespeare and African experience. His article is at once an oblique expression of carefully channelled rage, a Shakespearean endorsement of that anger, and political commentary.

For example, Themba tells a South Africanised version of *Julius Caesar*, a play historically popular among anti-colonial African elites across the continent. Or, as Themba puts it, the play was 'that ... starting point in the Shakespearean odyssey for many an African who has staggered through literacy'. He manages a laughing reference to the fraught history of literacy for Africans at the same time as he points to African achievements in this difficult sphere: 'There is a translation in Tswana by Sol Plaatje.' [13] In his précis, Themba mixes languages, registers, and themes, amalgamating colloquial American English with a 'Shakespearean' register and a touch of isiXhosa. In transposing Shakespeare's *Caesar* to a South African locale, Themba adds local resonance (the conspirators are men 'from the cities', thus invoking the long-standing tensions between rural and urban dwellers in the development of South Africa's urban locations):

> Apparently, Chief Kaiser Msi had trampled down the haughty heads of most of the lesser chiefs in the Transkei and left them licking their bruised ambitions ... He was so widely acclaimed by the rabble and the world at large that many of these disgruntled chieftains murmured:

> Why, man, he doth bestride the narrow world

Like a Colossus, and we petty men
Walk under his huge legs and peep about
To find ourselves dishonourable graves.

But there were other Xhosa, mostly from the cities, who resented the rapid rise of this upstart. They sought to clip his pinions, but the snag was that, being city men, it would have been hard for them to convince the tribesmen that it was in the holiest interest of the Transkei that Msi should be assassinated. A bright idea hit them! What they needed was a high-placed Xhosa, one everybody respected, one known to be honourable, to lead the conspiracy. And who else, they thought, but that dashing young gallant chief, Dilizintaba Sakwe ... As the Americans would say, they sold him the line of how Kaiser was ambitious, and his ambition threatened the weal of the Transkei, and how Kaiser had to die that Transkei might live ... On Ntsikana's Day ... the conspirators approached [Kaiser] as if they were his friends. They ... stabbed him, one after another, and when he saw Sakwe also as one of his killers, he cried out in anguish: 'Tixo, nawe, mntwanenkosi!' [God, you, my son!] ...

One thing that still reverberates in the Transkei is the magnificent speech said to have been made by a young Xhosa lawyer on the occasion of Kaiser's funeral ... His eloquence so roused the mob that factions forgot their feuds and went berserk in their passion to avenge Kaiser Msi.

Ah, me ... that is fantasy ... [14]

The juxtaposition of registers, formal and casual, slang and Shakespearean, ironically points to the apparent difference in generic registers between Shakespearean tragedy and African politics. On one level, Themba emphasises this apparent difference by his mock-regretful sigh, 'Ah, me ... that is fantasy.' (He might also be fantasising rather pointedly; it should be noted that Nelson Mandela was an eloquent 'young Xhosa lawyer' at this time.) However, the irony doubles back on itself, and *Julius Caesar* is seen to perfectly incorporate African stories and experiences. Most obviously, this illustration of the applicability of 'Shakespeare's' play serves to underscore the humanity shared by Africans and the original recipients of the best of the 'Western tradition', Themba's opening point. At the same time, by suggesting that there is a Shakespearean quality to African politics, Themba also implies that there is an African quality to Shakespeare's plays. Once again, Africans embody all that Shakespeare stands for.

And Themba himself embodies a Shakespearean truth about race relations. Making particularly brutal use of women's bodies ('A friend of mine tells me that if ever he got arrested for raping a white woman, he would tell the judge: "Your Honour, I'm aggrieved that anyone could ever imagine that I would ever be attracted by ... that ... Allow me to bring before the court a full-blooded African woman and I will show you where I am capable of rape ... "' [15]), he uses *Othello* to deride white masculinity and assert his own masculine power and his mastery of the tools of whiteness. He also makes chilling reference to lynching, while managing to profit from the toxic sexual politics which underlie such racist violence.

'That famous "act of immorality" committed by Othello and Desdemona fascinates me more than aught else', [16] he begins, again mixing registers (here, a reference to the legal language which policed intimacy during apartheid, and the Shakespearean flavour which makes the point he is about to explore, that his knowledge of Shakespeare allows him to outwit the white man's attempts to deny him white women). Iago doesn't care about the miscegenation he invokes to whip up Desdemona's household, Themba says. Rather, 'he knows that this thing that he is about to detonate touches the pack nigh and keenly. It is the most direct route to mob frenzy.' [17] It is white men, not black, who behave like animals, who act as a 'pack' and display 'herd animosity'. [18] Themba pushes the point about the sexual insecurity of white men, reformulating the putative sexual potency of black men on which it depends. '[L]imply, unconvincingly the white men about us try to cast their arrogance around, but it is oft so sickly pathetic that it raises more a smile than a scowl.' Crucially, it is his Shakespearean skill, again embedded in the sentence, which confirms at once his cultural and his sexual superiority, since, like Othello, Themba can beat the white man at his own game:

> With a little education, a little fluent English, a little know-how, a little self-assertion and a little desiring of the sweets of his life and the women ... We threaten his barest self-esteem. Moot, further, the fiction that we as savages are sexually more compelling and you have announced Armageddon. You do not have to whistle at a white girl passing by. Only the crude ones among us play it that way. Cultivate yourself into a superior being; grapple with something in their world and succeed ... Talk as if the high-brow things came naturally to you ... Then trembling whitedom

looks round at you with that curious mixed reaction of fear, wrath and horror. *Écrasez l'infame!*

It is just this that Othello went and done ... [19]

Both Themba and Othello are coconuts, versed in the language (or, as Themba displays here, languages) and the cultures of the white men who need, use, and fear them (Othello, like urban Africans, 'made himself indispensable to the state', which is 'Worse still' [20]). This coconuttiness adheres in linguistic and other competencies, but serves sexual purpose, as a wounded black masculinity fights back. Black men are not the savages; white men are, and black men are nevertheless still sexually superior. And in case the reader isn't clear on Themba's cultural and sexual prowess, he goes on to assure us that the white women he gets are not 'the scum, the what the boss wouldn't stand a-stinking in his back yard in any case', [21] but real Desdemonas:

> He hath achieved a maid
> That paragons description and wild fame;
> One that excels the quirks of blazoning pens,
> And in the essential vesture of creation
> Does tire the ingener.

Or, as the boys in Johannesburg would say: 'Nay, man, Boeta Can, you got yourself a Jewess that's got background and bodice; looks like the lord took special time off to make her ... ' For the boys are particular about what kind of a white girl you found yourself. [22]

Themba's use of *Othello* is in fact a brilliant demonstration of the sexual politics of the play, which hinges on Othello's believing that his sense of self as he has built it in the world of Venice depends on Desdemona's being a good woman of 'background', and not devalued 'scum'. Whether or not he meant to deconstruct Othello's masculinity in this way, Themba certainly is using Shakespeare's play and its hero's status in order to perform his own sexual and cultural virtuosity. The performance matters as a political point, as commentary on current events and as an assertion of human worth and dignity. Shakespeare is a tool with both personal and political edges. The coconuttiness Themba's writing instantiates is a heartfelt assertion of self-worth in a world which denies him all the markers of humanity and manhood. [23]

The authorising nature of the comparison set in motion by Sampson for the *Drum* writers clearly had great resonance. Lewis Nkosi, in his autobiography, *Home and Exile*, also wrote: 'Ultimately, it was the cacophonous, swaggering world of Elizabethan England which gave us the closest parallel to our own mode of existence; the cloak and dagger stories of Shakespeare; the marvelously gay and dangerous time of change in Great Britain came close to reflecting our own condition.' [24] The mythologised image of Elizabethan England is appropriated in the search for an idiom to express the conditions of life for people who were increasingly being treated as subhuman, and as de-culturated from their 'appropriate' 'tribal' identities, which apartheid legislated back into being as part of a divide-and-rule policy.

'Cloak and dagger stories': Bloke Modisane

William Bloke Modisane, too, claims Shakespeare, in order to both explain and authenticate himself as an African man. Modisane's autobiography, *Blame Me On History*, [25] is a harrowing account of life in early apartheid South Africa, leading up to Modisane's decision in 1959 to go into exile. His tone throughout the book attempts the debonair, ironic detachment typical of the *Drum* writers and exemplified by Themba, but most often collapses into bitterness and despair.

Modisane's complex performances of his acquisition of the culture about which he is scathingly ironic and for which he nonetheless yearns comprise some of the most painful sections of his autobiography. His use of Shakespeare must be seen as one of these performances, at once a demonstration of worth and a demand for recognition, and the legitimation of the ravaging emotions that accompanied the achievement of neither.

Modisane refers to Shakespeare throughout his autobiography, both in passing references and at length. He repeatedly makes the link between the effects of education and the position of what he calls 'a Caliban', thus making Caliban representative of a colonised group: 'If I am a freak it should not be interpreted as a failure of their education for a Caliban'; 'Bantu education [has been] ... described as the education for a Caliban'; 'Africans have protested against this system of education on the grounds that it is an education for Caliban'. [26]

In the first instance, where Modisane describes himself as a 'freak' because of his propensity for 'Western music, art, drama and philosophy', [27] his invocation of himself as 'a' Caliban is ironic. History, not education, is to blame for his freakishness, he says. [28] It is his inability to be the Caliban he is supposed by a racist system to be, that constitutes the 'problem'. Thereafter, Caliban stands for the subjugated 'native', taught to be subservient by the Prospero-establishment.

He makes use of *Hamlet* to exemplify the emotion which causes people to take part in riots, thus countering the image of a rampaging mob which so terrified the South African authorities and which was invoked to confirm the 'barbarity' of black people:

> Then it happened, I mean the action which has caused the death of many people in countless riots; it is not an act of bravery, of reckless courage, nor definitely one of stupidity. It is an action which shows man as a complicated set of responses capable – under normal circumstances – of reactions within a limited range of experiences, but beyond a certain limit of endurance of losing control of his rationale, shouting like Laertes:
>
> > To hell, allegiance! vows, to the blackest devil!
> > Conscience and grace, to the profoundest pit!
> > I dare damnation: – to this point I stand, –
> > That both the worlds I give to negligence,
> > Let come what comes; only I'll be revenged ... [29]

This rendering of the reasons for rioting places the responsibility for the violence firmly with the system and those who maintain it. Shakespeare's authority is invoked to emphasise the complex humanity of the individual forced by unbearable circumstance to extreme acts. The imperative to revenge, cast in this light, is heroic, proof of the fully developed manhood of, ultimately, Modisane himself. Modisane's manhood is fatally compromised by his inability to resort to violence in the face of apartheid repression, an inability exacerbated by the 'European' model of the liberal gentleman to which he responds so strongly. Modisane uses Shakespeare to solve this affective paradox:

> It has been impressed on me that only in the blood of Caesar could the conspirators prevent the abuse of power which might sway Caesar more than his reason; but it was Brutus who realised the margin between power and the physical man, warning that since the 'quarrel will bear no colour to the thing he is,' let us concern ourselves with the destruction of a symbol, which we hate, but not the man. Like Brutus, I am haunted by the immediacy, the direct presence of blood between oppression and the freedom which I must snatch. [30]

Throughout *Blame Me on History*, Modisane wrestles with the implications for his humanity if he kills white people in the name of the Struggle, and the implications for his manhood if he does not resist to the utmost of his capacity the injustices and humiliations of the system, implemented by those white people he needs to resist, and in which all white people are implicated. More directly here than in his use of Laertes, Brutus and Modisane are presented as experiencing the same, terrible, dilemma. They occupy a similar moral and heroic space. Modisane is thus a Shakespearean tragic hero – poetic, suffering, doomed: 'The whip lashes only at the will of the hand which is willed by the mind. Do I take the whip away or do I amputate the hand to remove the power to hurt others? This is the confrontation of Brutus.' [31] Like Othello, Modisane says, 'my worth cries out for recognition, even in place of acceptance, as it was said that Othello was respected and recognised but not accepted into Venetian society'. He quotes Roderigo's pejorative description of Othello in order to make the point that 'I resolved that if I could not delight and be loved by white South Africa, at least I should be feared'. [32] In a differently inflected way to Themba, Modisane is also choosing Othello's position, the only position open to him, in the Shakespearean drama that is apartheid South Africa, which accrues to itself some kind of 'masculine' power. Modisane is illustrating the worth he is denied by demonstrating, not only his knowledge of Shakespeare, but his status as coterminous with Shakespeare's tragic hero. He is claiming some kind of power, even if it is the power of being demonised and feared.

Modisane's painful identity struggle refracts the complicated interactions between class aspiration in a situation of racialised inequality and colonial education practices, and individual psychology (including masculinity and the relation between culture and identity) in these contexts. The Shakespeare he writes about, like Plaatje's, like Themba's, is reflective at once of personal ownership and of (intensified) protest that is both political and personal. It is marked by class and gender and a related experience of racialisation. This Shakespeare exemplifies the complicated coconuttiness it simultaneously enables and instantiates.

Shakespeare our contemporary?

Taking the similarities between their lives and the world of Shakespeare's plays as variously inflected starting points, Themba and Modisane demonstrate their intelligence in the terms prescribed by a dominant notion of what constitutes 'cultural worth'. The stupidity and brutality of the system that denies them equality then becomes patently obvious. This strategy became available in part through the construction of Elizabethan England and Sophiatown in the 1950s as similar spaces. But claiming a special connection to Shakespeare's time is not a strategy unique to an educated clique in 1950s South Africa. The link between Shakespeare's time and modern spaces of conflict is regularly repeated. Michael Yogev, in an analysis of how difference operated in his Shakespeare classes at the University of Haifa, suggests that 'contemporary Israel roughly parallels Elizabethan England'. Such a parallel allows him to insist upon the 'remarkabl[e] relevan[ce]' of Shakespeare to Israel. He therefore concludes: 'Shakespeare has never seemed more our contemporary.' [33] Similarly, in explicating their function in an American classroom, Michael Collins insists upon the essential and enduring moral worth of the plays: 'Shakespeare is still in some ways our contemporary.' [34] As Jonathan Holmes points out, this contradictory Shakespeare is at once both relevant to the present and informed by the authority of 'his' placement in the past, which guarantees 'his' abiding 'worth'. [35]

The overdetermined figure of 'our contemporary' Shakespeare, regardless of which of 'us' is speaking, and for whom, points to the weighting of what we might call 'common themes' raised by experiences of conflict and difference, as 'Shakespearean'. In other words, 'Shakespeare's' putative ability to represent the universally human is so encoded in our cultural vocabularies (where, neo-colonially, 'our' stands for a range of societies) that general human emotions are recognised as such *because* they are 'Shakespearean'. Thus, as Holmes suggests, the apparent universal humanism of Shakespeare does not automatically ensure a human-rights perspective, where 'difference' is respected without weighting one culture over another. Following his analyses of Janet Suzman's South African production of *Othello* in 1987, and Antony Sher and Gregory

Doran's 1995 production of *Titus Andronicus*, Holmes concludes that attempts to invoke Shakespeare to comment on the rights of oppressed South Africans can be spectacularly unsuccessful.

Comparisons that seek historical specificity – the similarities between Elizabethan England and a modern locale – in fact, rely on an implicit sense of the 'universalism and transcendence of Shakespeare'. [36] Of the attempts to invoke this understanding of Shakespeare in order to create human rights theatre in South Africa, Holmes comments: 'Suzman and Doran work to expunge all otherness and difference from their writing in favour of a universal humanist sameness which in reality is the province of a few western Europeans.'[37]

As much as it can be used effectively to protest against the abuse of human rights, Shakespeare's universal authority can be invoked to overwrite difference even as it tries to oppose oppression based on the entrenchment of a hierarchy of difference. Thus, while writers like Plaatje, Themba, Nkosi, and Modisane invoke the universal humanity understood to be best expressed by Shakespeare in order to insist in part on the equal humanity of black South Africans, the tool of Shakespeare's universal status is double-edged: the other side of propounding universality is the disavowal of the systemic construction, weighting, and concomitant experience of difference. Sampson's liberal view, which is able to see difference only when it is cast in recognisable terms, renders Sophiatown's violence familiar and, ultimately, enjoyable. The pain of living in Sophiatown, as documented by Modisane, is excised from Sampson's picture, as are the socio-political causes that resulted in the development of urban slums and the nihilistic lifestyles of their desperate inhabitants. [38]

Liberalism, following especially the work of Steve Biko, [39] the leader of Black Consciousness in the 1970s, has a specific

South African meaning. In part, liberalism in South Africa has been identified (not without some simplification) largely as the sphere of the English, [40] and, accordingly, as having a link to what Shakespeare has been made to stand for in South Africa. This is no simple signification. Allowing Shakespeare to represent liberal aspirations and practices in South Africa means both that 'he' denotes a humanist, human foil to the dehumanising apartheid state, and that 'he' was complicit in apartheid education practices, [41] entrenching and naturalising 'white' privilege by encoding a particular history and literature as the best the world has to offer, and by palliating apartheid privilege through weak and empty expressions of theoretical equality unmatched in social practice.

'Because of the violence': Antony Sher's liberal Shakespeare

This kind of liberalism's tendency to be able to see only what it already knows, in spite of genuine attempts at well-intentioned interventions, is clearly in evidence in Sher and Doran's published account of their controversial production of *Titus Andronicus*, coyly titled *Woza Shakespeare!* in reference to the famous anti-apartheid play *Woza Albert!* Sher, one of South Africa's most famous expatriate sons, returns here periodically to stage performances, in 2009 again of Shakespeare. [42] In *Woza Shakespeare!*, Sher and Doran also invoke the 'connections' between the two times and places to explain their choice of play for the Market Theatre: Titus 'sort of makes sense in Africa ... I suppose because of the violence.' [43] The shared 'violence' of the two societies is repeatedly invoked in this text, as are '[t]he rhythms ... and beauty and *humour* in both'. [44] In this formulation, the connection between Elizabethan England and the putatively essential 'African' again resides in a shared premodernity that can be celebrated as a kind of glorious, brutal chaos. The ultimate valuation of such a world is made clear in Sher's novel *The Feast*, [45] written after his experience of staging *Titus* in South Africa. The story of a white thespian trying to work in a fictitious post-independence African country characterises the place as dangerous and poverty-ridden, its culture as maimed and mutilating, and its leadership as corrupt and dictatorial. *Titus* is thematically invoked in this novel.

Furthermore, Sher's outraged response to the criticism his South Africanised *Titus* elicited in the country revealed the limits of his liberal intentions: Sher's Shakespeare was intended as a gift of culture to benighted South Africans, whose inability to appreciate his interpretation was confirmation of their own inadequacies and not of the quality of his production. This is taken up in chapter three.

Sher and Doran are careful to limit their critique of their South African audience to the white members. For example, a hostile interviewer is accounted for by Sher:

> I've met his type before in this country. Always white, often journalists ... the press ... might still be run by the same people, still confused as to why anyone was ashamed of the old South Africa.

> So far, my homecoming has been marked by two general responses. Blacks tend to say, 'Welcome home, thanks for your efforts abroad.' Whites, like Dr Whatsisname today, tend to say, 'Oh *you're* back.' [46]

The gratitude of black South Africans serves to prove both the superior moral quality of the victims of apartheid and the worth of Sher's Shakespearean undertaking. Also lurking behind the need to affirm African appreciation of Shakespeare is the anxiety of 'relevance', which has played such a divisive part in the history of South African debates about literature in the classrooms of schools and universities. [47]

In part, as I go on to argue in the next chapter, Sher's anxiety of relevance is a self-anxiety. If Plaatje, Themba, and Modisane are kinds of South African coconut whose Shakespeares speak to their historical positionalities and personal journeys, then Sher is perhaps another kind of coconut. If South African cultural history contains figures of black men who negotiate a relationship with English and Englishness through its most famous son, it also contains people like Antony Sher, a white South African who must manage the meaning of Englishness and its relation to Africanness in a deeply personal, as well as performative, manner. Sher's Shakespeare is every bit as 'relevant' to post-apartheid South African identity positions and their imbrication with race and class. But not because a homogenised 'Africanness' is 'like' – as violent as, as premodern as – Elizabethan England.

CHAPTER 3

Tony's Will:

Titus Andronicus in South Africa, 1995

This chapter examines the writing about a production of *Titus Andronicus*, which starred expatriate South African Anthony Sher. The production was co-conceived with, and directed by, Sher's British partner, Gregory Doran. Originally staged in South Africa in 1995, the production subsequently toured England and Spain with its South African cast. The process of staging *Titus*, and the two men's responses to critiques of the play, were documented in *Woza Shakespeare!*, published in 1996, apparently the diary kept by Sher and Doran during the production's various runs. The production was filmed at the Market Theatre by the South African Broadcasting Corporation, so a representation of Sher and Doran's play survives. Reviews of the play and the book from both South Africa and England were numerous, which means ample material documenting the reception of the play is also extant.

From the reviews it is possible to develop an idea of a range of audience members' responses to the play. In addition, the personal record that is *Woza Shakespeare!* offers an opportunity to trace the production and reception of a very particular Shakespeare production, in a very particular locale, from the point of view of its principal producers and its lead actor. What becomes clear from an investigation of the play's incarnation in South Africa in 1995, and an exploration of Sher's extended textual self-fashioning, is that particular constructions of the 'Shakespearean' and of the 'South African' are at work in the various texts that comprise the traces this production has left behind. *Titus Andronicus* at the Market Theatre in newly post-apartheid South Africa becomes a vehicle for Sher as a white sometimes-South African to search for an identity. Some of the strategies available to his identity formation are enabled by 'Shakespeare' (the icon) and the play *Titus Andronicus*, as both become conduits through which Sher channels his sense of self. 'South Africa' and particular notions of the 'African' are equally available as ideological constructions, and are invoked in a particular relation to Sher's sense of 'England' and 'English culture'.

Sher's work on *Titus Andronicus* chronicles some of the meanings of 'Shakespeare' for particular identity positions in a neo-colonial world, and particularly for certain groups of white people in post-apartheid South Africa. As such it instantiates a different version of South African coconuttiness, a version which is equally reliant on binary formations. This kind of coconuttiness may not perform a black person's aspirations to 'whiteness' as a signifier of class mobility, modernity, or cultural or social worth. But it equally relies on the assumption that English whiteness is better than a version of, here, South Africanness. This kind of coconuttiness has a different relation to race, but a no less real one for all that. If anything, Sher's performances in South Africa in 1995 bespeak the truly reductive meanings behind the invocation of the coconut, meanings I have been contesting so far. Sher, in other words, is far more revealing of the original cultural politics of the coconut than those other Englished South

Africans I have discussed. It is no coincidence, I think, that the figure of the liberal white man is a more accurate incarnation of, more directly profiting and profiteering from, a binary identity politics, than any more apparently 'traditional' coconut.

First performed in 1594, and very popular in its own time, the play, *Titus Andronicus*, has been notoriously badly received until comparatively recently. *Titus* has been famously maligned by, amongst others, Samuel Johnson ('The barbarity of the spectacles, and the general massacre which are here exhibited, can scarcely be conceived tolerable to any audience' [1]); Edward Ravenscroft ('the play is "rather a heap of rubbish than a structure"' [2]); T.S. Eliot ('who called it "one of the stupidest and most uninspired plays ever written"' [3]); and John Dover Wilson ('the play is "like some broken-down cart, laden with bleeding corpses from an Elizabethan scaffold, and driven by an executioner from Bedlam dressed in cap and bells"'; [4] it is '"a huge joke" ... in which Shakespeare watched the groundlings "gaping ever wider to swallow more as he tossed them bigger and bigger gobbets of sob-stuff and raw beef-steak"' [5]). That the play appeals more to the twentieth century than to the periods intervening between its own time and modernity is suggested in its performance history: 'there have been more productions ... of *Titus Andronicus* since 1923 than during any comparable period in the play's earlier stage history'. [6] Despite (or perhaps because of) their ability to tolerate the violence, [7] the play's grotesqueries have often been problematic for twentieth-century audiences, who tend to laugh at some of the scenes of violence. [8]

Before the production under discussion, the only other performance on the continent was the 1970 production directed by Dieter Reible, translated into Afrikaans by Breyton Breytenbach. [9] Why, then, choose to stage *Titus* in newly post-apartheid South Africa? Given the opportunity to stage anything they liked at the Market, as Sher and Doran were, [10] why choose Shakespeare?

The reason is partly fortuitous. Doran had been due to direct the play in Nigeria, but during the pair's initial trip to South Africa to run a series of workshops, the scheduled production was cancelled due to '[t]he political crisis in that country'. [11] So, having made the decision to stage a Shakespeare in South Africa, Doran and Sher 'decide to propose *Titus* to the Market', citing the reasons whose history and logic we have explored in the previous chapter:

> I think it's a play about our capacity for cruelty, and our capacity for survival; about the way violence breeds violence; about the search for justice in a brutal universe. It's about a world I [Doran] recognise around me, particularly here in Africa. [12]

And:

> Whereas the scene [where Titus amputates his own hand] can be absurd and revolting elsewhere, doing the play here in South Africa, a society which has suffered decades of atrocious violence, a strange reversal occurs. The acts of brutality, instead of being gratuitous or extreme, seem only too familiar ... [13]

Sher and Doran also say they chose Shakespeare because of their experience of working with South African accents during their workshops. They find that their attempts to offer an alternative to the 'vocal imperialism' of the received pronunciation of Shakespeare are resisted by local actors, and they take this to be a sign of the colonisation of the South African mind by

British 'perceptions of language' regarding how Shakespeare is supposed to sound. [14] Sher identifies with this struggle, and responds to the South African inflections when Shakespeare is spoken by the actors in their everyday voices (not 'an assumed English accent' [15]):

> I'm on the edge of my seat, fascinated and tense –
> because, of course, that's *me* on the stage. I've spent
> a lifetime burying my South Africanness, in the
> belief that good acting, proper acting and certainly
> Shakespearian acting, has to be English.
>
> As soon as Greg encourages the actors to try again,
> using their own accent, their own energy, their
> own *centre*, they transform. Suddenly they become
> the actors who amazed audiences around the world
> [in non-Shakespearian productions] ... with their
> rawness, their passion.
>
> And now I sit there thinking, this could be me, this
> could be *me*.
>
> What's it going to be like, playing Shakespeare in
> an accent like this? – an accent that isn't all smooth
> and rounded, but full of muscle and edges. An earth
> accent, a root accent, instead of one that floats and
> flitters around in the air. [16]

The summary description of the multiple South African accents that must have been present in the workshop resonates with an old construction of what Doran above denotes 'Africa': a continent which can be understood as a single country, with a homogenous identity characterised by a relationship to the earth (the key terms above are 'earth' and 'root') that is less modulated by the processes of civilisation (having 'rawness' and 'passion'). Inevitably, this characterisation acquires meaning in a binary relation: 'English' is 'smooth and rounded', it 'floats and flitters'. It is airy, ethereal, intellectual, in opposition to Africanness's muscular physicality. Sher later comments of his Afrikaans-accented Titus, 'The accent ... [is] allowing me to do things with my voice which more typically, as an actor, I do with my body.' [17]

Given the colonial framework of such logic, it is not surprising to find scattered throughout *Woza Shakespeare!*, in countless throwaway comments, the assumption that Britain is the norm and standard, to which South Africa should aspire (for example: 'How can the local theatre-going public afford to be blasé about a performance like this – which even London hasn't seen yet?'; [18] 'I want to tell them how much this means to me, to see all these South African actors here ... – here at the Royal National Theatre for God's sake! ... '; [19] 'I realise that this is not the RSC or the National Theatre, but I'm unprepared for the level of inefficiency ...' [20]). This standard colonial binary relation, here cast as England/South Africa, [21] through which Sher, particularly, modulates his experience of staging *Titus* in Johannesburg, tends to collapse *Woza Shakespeare!*'s representations into stereotypes.

It is in the assumptions about accent evident in the production, and in Sher and Doran's use of race in their casting and characterisation, that stereotypes are most evidently perpetuated. As I have already suggested, accent is important to Sher as a marker of identity: '"I lost my own South African accent twenty-six years ago when I left here to go overseas to train as an actor. I was embarrassed by it and I used to disguise it. And I think I lost my relationship with my own voice."' [22] Through his Afrikaans Titus, that relationship is 'nurtured back', [23] but in

Sher's emotional celebration of how it feels to do Shakespeare in an 'authentic' South African accent, the contradictions inherent to many issues of essentialised identity politics emerge. Sher's Titus is an Afrikaner; this is not Sher's native accent. Similarly, Dorothy Ann Gould's Tamora speaks in a 'poor white' accent, [24] one she developed while playing in Fugard's *Hello and Goodbye.* Indeed, many of the main actors are putting on accents to do their earthy and 'authentic' South African Shakespeare as much as they would be if they reverted to the English accents Sher and Doran decry as inauthentic. More than this, what results from this assumption of identity positions as designated by accent – 'Afrikaner'; 'poor white'; 'coloured' [25] (the association of 'poor white' with 'coloured', in that Tamora is Queen of the otherwise coloured Goths, has a specific and fraught history of which Sher and Doran seem to be ignorant [26]) – is a reductive stereotyping of a series of apartheid-inflected identities at a time when South Africans were uncertainly adjusting to what it meant to be post-apartheid. This, and not the cultural retardation of which Sher accuses (white) South Africans repeatedly, was likely to have had something to do with the negative response his production received in Johannesburg. [27] It possibly also explains, in part, why the British audience embraced it, recognisably South African as it was to them. [28]

South Africa and England

One of the notable elements of this production is its reliance on specific understandings of 'the South African' which it attempts to deploy interpretatively. The production's use of 'the South African' relies on Sher's relationship to this construction. Sher's binary construction of Britishness and South Africanness, with its implicit hierarchy, emerges from the book (and thus, presumably, from the experience of staging the production in South Africa), as the result of a process of identification. This process follows Sher's explicit vacillation between what he understands as two separate identities. He begins *Woza Shakespeare!* by marking a return to the possibility of being South African, following the demise of apartheid, by recounting the reclaiming of his South African passport. [29] South Africanness becomes something he says he can finally be proud of and want to identify with. In addition, both he and Doran comment on his bad year in England, with 'a series of [work-related] disappointments': Sher lost two parts in a row because he wasn't considered big-name enough. [30] 'I've had such a bloody awful year work-wise back home that maybe it's time to ... ,' he tells Doran, and, 'This country [South Africa] ... it's starting to smell cleaner than home. Mind you, where is home now?'[31] In his autobiography some four years later, Sher is explicit about feeling 'fairly disgruntled with England in September 1994 [because of his professional disappointments] when we flew to South Africa – and this was a place of miracles.' [32] In other words, his emotional return to his 'homeland' coincides with a sense of disillusionment with his 'adopted land', which is related to feeling under-appreciated. When *Titus* wins awards in Britain and controversy in South Africa, he concludes, 'Hey, maybe my career ain't so bad here' in England. [33] On opening night in England, he comments:

> A different shiver goes up my spine as I do the opening speech today:
>> Cometh Andronicus ...
>> To re-salute his country with his tears ...

The country which I'm now thinking of as *mine*, and
which I'm re-saluting with my 'tears of true joy' –
and with this production – is England.

For me, one of the most valuable things to come out
of the Jo'burg experience is the chance to reappraise
my career here in England and, quite frankly, to
thank my cotton socks for it! [34]

Placing oneself at the centre of the meanings one makes of the
world is a human impulse. However, what Sher does is enlist
South Africa as a symbolic aspect of his personal identity
struggle; part of this process entails reinscribing a colonial value
system which makes particular, and, for post-colonial theorists,
familiar, use of Shakespeare. Sher and Doran expect Shakespeare
to occupy a specific position in the South African cultural
landscape, and take it as a negative reflection on South Africa that
'he' does not necessarily or automatically guarantee audiences
and/or their grateful appreciation. When they encounter the
reality that Shakespeare in South Africa is predominantly a
school setwork, they interpret this as further evidence of South
African provinciality. [35] Their repeated cry is, 'Thanks a bunch –
why did nobody warn us?' [36]

Woza Shakespeare! is presented as a diary, as a series of
'portraits ... of their relationship, both professional and personal'
(as recounted in the book's blurb). It thus promises a glimpse
into the thoughts and feelings of two people which is interesting
at least partly because it offers an insight into the private lives
of two *famous* people. The conflation of the personal and the
performative is made clear in the book's list of 'Dramatis
Personae, [37] where 'real' people are listed as 'characters' in
Sher and Doran's personal and professional 'real life drama'

(as the blurb states). *Woza Shakespeare!*'s diary format, with its present-tense voice, seems to offer an unmediated and authentic document of a process while at the same time making use of highly scripted techniques such as foreshadowing and dramatic irony. The same implicit claim to authentic experience is offered in the presentation of South Africa and South Africans to the assumed British audience (prices in South African rands are converted into British pounds in parentheses in the text; comments are addressed to a British reader: 'These are the Vita Awards [South Africa's equivalent of the Oliviers].' [38]). The book offers snippets and summaries of South African history ('The Cultural Boycott: a brief history' [39]), and sociological analyses of post-apartheid South Africa and its peoples ('Some people fear that here [in the student riots at Wits] in microcosm they are witnessing the eventual fate of the country' [40]), as well as, finally, a very public judgement on the state of theatre and accordingly of 'culture' in the country:

> When we complain ... about the lack of publicity, [Mike Maxwell] says, 'The problem seems to be that Tony's work isn't known here.' Greg said, 'But what about his *reputation* – that's known, surely?' 'Maybe, but it's what I've said before. Having been excluded from the outside world for so long, South Africans are not that interested in it' ...
>
> South Africans have lost interest in the outside world. I mean, modesty aside, surely Greg and my joint experience of British theatre, and particularly of Shakespeare, should have been of more interest to Wits's drama department ...? [41]

To which attitude reviewer Stephen Gray replied, 'South Africans ... have become bored with mouldy royals patronising them.' [42] Most of these generalised contentions (Who are 'some people'?) and simplified overviews of the country's history are given without sources. Some are incorrect, and many are problematic: Sher denotes the taxis that carry the majority of South Africans to and from work 'black taxis', a casually racist term used by some white South Africans and here presented as 'the' name of the method of transportation. The clown is played as 'a little Coloured pigeon fancier from the Cape Flats, a klonkie who can't say his Rs'. [43] 'Klonkie' is a derogatory word for a coloured person which, while available to be reclaimed, like 'nigger', is a word white people need to use with care. The representation of a lower-class coloured person who speaks with a bray is a stereotype. Sher and Doran provide incorrect facts about the Market; [44] and about what languages are spoken by which South Africans, placing a Sesotho speaker as a Transkei local (where the language spoken is isiXhosa). [45] The book thus claims an authority to represent South Africa to an English audience in ways similar, and similarly careless, that the production itself did.

In a book that claims to document the process of a Shakespeare production, what is documented is Sher's process of identification, and his eventual opting for Englishness and England as the preferred location for his sense of, and thus him-, self. In the extract from *Woza Shakespeare!* quoted on page 75, Sher watches South African actors struggle to speak Shakespeare. His response – 'of course, that's *me* on the stage ... this could be me, this could be *me*' – illustrates how the act of identification can become a kind of appropriation.

In seeking to authenticate his responses to South Africa, Sher performs another kind of appropriation. This is important to note here because it helps to authorise his presentation of South Africa to the British audience of the book: 'I'm an outsider, belonging to three minority groups (Jewish, gay, white South African), so my view of things is always askew; I'll never see them as Mr Normal does.' [46] The disingenuous conflation of white South Africanness and Jewishness with the minority identity of gayness overlooks socio-economic allocations of power. Being a white South African may make one a numerical minority group, but it is the group historically, and in many ways still, in possession of social and economic power. In the context of apartheid – and indeed, post-apartheid – South Africa, the suggestion that Jewishness can be separated from the privileges of whiteness is arguable. Elsewhere, in an interview, Sher makes the claim that, being Jewish and gay, he 'must have connected, even subconsciously, with knowing to some extent what the black and coloured people were experiencing'. [47] This ignores the enormous difference between being white (albeit gay or Jewish) and being black in apartheid South Africa and is again a kind of appropriation. Sher's inability to see the South African in terms other than those that mirror himself results in an attempt at a kind of colonisation. It is no wonder, then, that his documentation of his experience of producing *Titus* reflects a kind of colonial logic in the sense it makes of the South African response to the play. It is no wonder, either, that he experiences the country's theatre-going public's refusal to mirror his sense of himself, as an intensely personal rejection.

The binary understanding of meaning, where the 'African' is contrasted to the 'English', and the appropriation of 'African' landscapes, voices, and experiences to stage a process for the white 'self', are colonial positions. These positions are given valency by Sher's status as a Shakespearean actor – as an authorised purveyor of culture – and by this production, a Shakespeare play. The mutually reinforcing status of both is assumed in the book, as we have seen in Sher and Doran's attitudes to the South African responses to their presence and production.

Thus it is no surprise that the other reason for settling on *Titus* is that the character seems to echo Sher's experience, fortuitously including the disappointment of the returning hero's hopes: Doran says to Sher, '"Do you know what your first lines as a professional actor on a South African stage will be?" I quote them to him: "Hail Rome ... / Lo ... / Cometh Andronicus, bound with laurel boughs, / To re-salute his country with his tears, / Tears of true joy for his return to Rome." "That's you," I say. "You're coming back to re-salute your country!"' [48] Sher and Doran play repeatedly on the significance of these opening lines, and on Sher's 'violent surprise' at his reception in South Africa. (The book's blurb makes use of them; Doran says of rehearsals: 'Today we get to Titus's first entrance and when Tony finally has to utter those first few words about re-saluting his country with his tears, neither he nor I have any difficulty producing the goods';[49] Doran's opening-night card to Sher reads: '*Dearest Tones ... "Cometh Andronicus bound in laurel boughs to resalute his country with his tears". Welcome home*'; [50] Sher cries: 'I can't bear this ... I feel completely bloody bruised ... What the hell happened to my triumphant homecoming? It was exactly like Titus's. Just one shock after another'). [51] Shakespeare's play becomes the vehicle for expressing Sher's personal journey, and South Africa becomes the backdrop against which this personal odyssey acquires meaning, by opposition. Such a use of a European notion of 'Africa' was identified first by Chinua Achebe in relation to the functioning of the Congo and Congolese people in *Heart of Darkness*. [52]

What I will call the 'Conrad effect' undercuts the primary reason given by Sher and Doran for staging *Titus*. By cutting and pasting, Marcus is given a final, reconciliatory word with which to close the play: 'O let me teach you how to knit again / This scattered corn into one mutual sheaf ... ' In the synopsis of the production for the Market Theatre programme, we are told that the play ends with 'Marcus ... consider[ing] how to begin healing the wounds of a society devastated by violence and atrocity'. This is an obvious attempt to find parallels between the play and newly post-apartheid South Africa. There is no reason why a play by Shakespeare is the most appropriate vehicle for a statement on reconciliation. As the shifting of the speech from Act V scene iii to the end of the play suggests, Doran and Sher went out of their, and the play's, way to make this point. [53] Ultimately, under this formulation, the play's appropriateness as a statement to the 'new' South Africa relies on an implicit understanding of Shakespeare's cultural value. But this understanding of Shakespeare invokes a notion of cultural value that has its own, particular, history, and has specific implications for the African Other on which it in part relies, as indeed is clear in the workings of the representations in *Woza Shakespeare!*

Stereotyping Shakespeare

The stereotyping is explicitly racial. 'We're thinking of playing the Andronici as Afrikaners. Titus's family are of old Roman stock, with a self-righteous belief in their own importance. Like the Afrikaner nation, they are God-fearing and pure-bred', says Doran at the beginning of the play's conceptualisation [54] (the statement that Afrikaners are 'pure-bred' is another historical inaccuracy, and also a repetition of the apartheid strategies used in the name of separatism). Watching the first anniversary of the elections on television, Sher comments: 'So strange to see the podium full of war-horses from the old police force and army (a squad of Tituses), hefty, white-moustached Afrikaner generals.' [55] Both actors playing Lucius are chosen in part for their resemblance to rugby players. [56] With his military uniform and moustache, the actor who played Lucius in South Africa, Martin le Maitre, looks like a member of the apartheid SA National Defence Force; indeed, he is meant to be played 'as a hard-line man of war, a reactionary, racist, his father's son'. [57] This is the man in whose hands Rome is supposed to be safely delivered into a better future, leaving South Africans with a heartening message of the importance of reconciliation. By playing the Andronici according to stereotypical notions of Afrikanerdom, Sher and Doran make it impossible to read the play symbolically or allegorically as a statement for hopeful change, while simultaneously inviting precisely a reading that seeks for symbolic meaning in the play's casting.

Because of *Woza Shakespeare!*, we have a record of the thought processes that went into the characterisation and casting of the play. Sher and Doran think explicitly about race during this period of the play's conceptualisation: 'The play deals with issues of race and therefore we do need to be precise about the colour of actors we choose.' [58] They offer minute detail on the racial identities of their actors (to the extent of describing the racial features of some actors in some detail – so, for example, Lesley Fong's colouredness is situated alongside his Chinese features), and give reasons for their choices accordingly: 'Aaron has to be isolated in his blackness. Saturninus and Tamora have to be white, otherwise there would be no scandal when Tamora produces a black child.' [59] At the same time, the Queen of the Goths can be white, and her sons and subjects coloured, because 'we know Tamora has a penchant for black men'. [60] Bassianus, too, is played by a coloured actor, as, more problematically (again given a particular representational history where 'Cape Coons' are figures of fun), is the Clown. Paulus Kuoape can only be cast as the young Lucius once they find 'a way of changing the Boy in Act IV, so that he doesn't have to be Lucius's son'. [61] This way entails cutting all the boy's lines. [62]

The Goth brothers, played as coloured gangsters with their butterfly knives and jackrolling (gang-raping) behaviour invoke stereotypes perpetuated in the media and long acknowledged as seriously problematic. [63] At the same time as they are specifically marked as 'coloured', the qualities associated with the Goths are 'elementary' and 'primitive'. [64] The war dances they perform are modelled on the haka, 'that ape-like display', [65] an interpretation of a Zulu attack, and a *ratieb* ('a type of ritual dance, performed in the Malay communities of Cape Town' [66]). This results in a mishmash of faux 'African' sounds and movements,[67] whose contradictory claims to 'authenticity' (Zulu, Maori, coloured: a generic, highly masculinised, racialised Other) demonstrate Sher and Doran's reductive notions of racial difference in South Africa.

The ill-thought-through stereotyping continues: to stage Titus's first mad scene, the actors are sent onto the streets of Johannesburg to observe the homeless, in order to play what Sher designates as the 'Dump People'. [68] At the end of Act I a short scene is added where the invading Goths loot and riot because: '"What happens in Rome is just what all the whities feared would happen after the Elections here," someone says. "Like the looting in Bop[69] ... Terrible!"' [70] Accordingly, this section of the play, titled by the cast 'The Rise to Power', [71] plays out this fear, complete with 'a jaunty tune with echoes of Cape "Coon Carnival" music ... in about thirty seconds of stage time we see the Goths take over Rome'. [72] In what ways does this stagecraft develop or contribute to a coherent conceptualisation of the play? With the Andronici as Afrikaner stalwarts (standing for 'whites'), how can this scene of looting darkies be anything but simplistic and offensive, whichever way one leans politically? At best this is a crude attempt to bait white conservatives, but even on that level the concept falls short, given Sher and Doran's insistence on retaining racial identities. So Tamora's whiteness confounds this allegory here, as does the relation between colouredness and blackness in the way the play is staged, where Aaron's blackest villainy is somehow contextualised by apartheid racism, and the position of barbarian is allocated to the coloured subject, until the alliance with the uber-boereseun which excludes Aaron from the future of Rome.

The production does beg the question of its racialised analogy. One can't help feeling that Sher and Doran are dancing blithely unaware in a minefield. Their ignorance is particularly unacceptable given their self-proclaimed roles as presenters of the country to their British audience. Sher and Doran insist that the play's setting and the playing of the Andronici as Afrikaners, and the Goths as coloured South Africans, and the peripheral characters as 'bergies' (homeless people), is not to be taken literally. [73] If we take Doran at his word ('we are simply using what we've got', he innocently states in the Market Theatre programme's 'Director's Note', as though 'we' share the same starting points, and as if the racial assumptions arising from apartheid South Africa were there for the unproblematic perpetuating), what we are left with is the general idea that violence suits Africa, and that blackness is a sign of barbarity.

Sher and Doran disavow the racialised casting and characterisation when the contradictions of their conceptualisation begin to show. Sher recounts an exchange with the Royal Shakespeare Company's artistic director, Terry Hands, during the production's subsequent British run:

'It's probably my fault,' he says without conviction, 'but I was confused by the first half. The trouble is, I think very politically. So I couldn't work out what the parallels were.'

I smile back. 'Yes, one or two other people have made the same mistake. Trying to simplify it too much.'

He laughs. 'And I was very confused by your Terre'Blanche look.'

'Terre'Blanche? It's meant to be Spike Milligan.' [74]

In interviews with the British press, both Sher and Doran persist in refusing any direct political parallels. By the time they wrote *Woza Shakespeare!*, Doran was clear on the interpretative reasoning behind their production:

> We want Marcus's [final] words to resonate with the audience, for them to hear the echo [with reconciliation in the new South Africa]. I'm anxious that we go no further. Otherwise we would be ... trying too hard to apply a relevance which the play does not admit ... We have chosen to do the play in this way in order to liberate it, to make it accessible and relevant not in specific, but in general terms. We are certainly not presenting allegory. [75]

Given their repeated insistences that *Titus* was specifically relevant to South African history, Sher and Doran's disavowal of the racial allegorisation suggested by their interpretation seems, at best, naïve, and helps to account for the negative reception the play elicited from some South African audiences.

Potential *Tituses*

There are multiple concerns, thematic and generic, in *Titus Andronicus* which could provide points of convergence with newly post-apartheid South African society, particularly a South Africa discussing the possibility of a Truth and Reconciliation Commission on the one hand, and drafting a new constitutional framework on the other, if such a comparison was deemed necessary. Most obviously, in its opening scene, the play points out different political models of statehood, and might be seen to be commenting on methods of governance in a shifting political arena. The play might enable the staging of a warning about the need for legal restitution of wrongs, in order to prevent cycles of violence from contaminating a state that has just acquired new leadership. Linked to its exploration of modes of rulership is the question of the definition of justice, the state's role in meting it out, and the functioning of state-sanctioned violence and personal revenge. Deborah Willis suggests that the play's genre, revenge tragedy, is typically concerned with the difficulties of managing traumatic experience when the state cannot be trusted to deliver justice, while at the same time honour systems that rely on inter-family warfare exacerbate violent acts, resulting in an increased number of traumatised innocents. [76] Louise Noble explores the notions of violence as a disease, and as pollution therapy in the world of the play: 'in an extraordinary attempt to restore political stability to Rome, horrifying acts of revenge are performed as harsh homeopathic remedies'. [77] Because there is no possibility of 'legal restitution', 'personal justice ... becomes a unifying motif of the play'. [78] This violence is brutally enacted on bodies; the bodies of children and the bodies of women acquire particular meaning in this regard.[79]

Indeed, 'the misogyny of *Titus Andronicus* is strongly overdetermined'. [80] This is one reason why the play is both a curious choice for Sher and Doran's purposes, and a potentially fruitful vehicle for the exploration of gender violence in South African societies. However, they overlook both the pitfalls and the potentials, creating instead a racially indeterminate Tamora (despite their careful rationale to account for her whiteness, they describe her as 'very sexy, slightly Oriental' [81]) who may invoke all the worst stereotypes of rampant 'coloured' oversexualisation, [82] and an irritatingly smug and passive Lavinia, who enacts stereotypes of the white colonial woman. Jennifer Woodburne's Lavinia is, first, a snobbish, prissy 'Afrikaner princess' [83] and then a slavering, tottering rag doll. Her rape is enacted on a shop dummy, a staging which literally reduces the female body to object. In discussion, too, Sher and Doran offer a profoundly misogynist interpretation of Lavinia's rape and mutilation. When asked why Titus murders Lavinia, for instance, Sher replied: 'She's a sick dog ... She needs to be put down.' [84]

Titus can be read as deconstructing the civilised/barbarian binary, [85] thus revealing the contingent nature of these categories. It famously insists on the location of barbarism within Rome. The play could offer the opportunity to engage with colonial and apartheid constructions of cultural otherness and its related 'racial' difference along these weighted lines. Certainly, the most powerful and moving moment in Sher and Doran's production is Sello Maake ka Ncube as Aaron's exclamation, 'Is black so base a hue?' The affective power of this line in this production comes not from its moment in the play, but from this production's location in space and time, and from the meaning of the actor's body accordingly.

With its strong classical influences the play explores how Empire is founded on rape, and that in the violence of its founding, Empire sows the seeds of its own destruction. [86] In 1995, it could be staged as an illustration of a disintegrating apartheid/colonial empire, and/or a warning about a new African empire (certainly in Sher's subsequent novel, *The Feast*, [87] all the standard Western fears and stereotypes about post-independence Africa are endorsed in this dystopian vision). *Titus* can offer a warning on the need to come to terms with the past; on revenge and its tolls on civic and personal coherence. It can offer a lesson on the processes of Othering, and a rather bleak assessment of how different cultures or families are equally prone to such processes. It can be used to discuss a patriarchal use of female bodies in a society riven by factional enmity. But when the reason given for staging the play in post-apartheid South Africa is that violence is typically African, then other representational systems and cultural assumptions come into (the) play. In the interpretative decisions made by Sher and Doran, and in the ways these decisions were translated into staging and characterisation, the play's potential to engage with the society in which it was placed was replaced by something that revealed instead preconceived notions of the 'South African', explored as part of the personal journey of the play's main player. Antony Sher became the protagonist of *Titus Andronicus*, and his relationship with South Africa became the main body of the action. Sher's inability to see other than from his own centre of experience is more than the narcissism of the great actor; it is a typical element of liberalism. His sense of entitlement is more than the result of his successful career; it is typical of a certain aspect of white identity formation. [88]

Further, once South African reviewers and audiences began to respond negatively to the production, Sher in particular moved the debate from the realm of theatre criticism to the realm of identity politics, merging the two in ways which reveal the intersection between identity as a performance requiring an audience, ethnicity, ego, whiteness, and an old colonial construction of otherness.

Critical responses to the production

According to Sher, even long after the fact, critics who adore the production have something worthwhile to say. Anyone else is, at best, stupid and unimaginative: 'Some of the critics raved, some were confused by the South African accents and settings. Surely Shakespeare should be posh, operatic, *British*? Surely Shakespeare shouldn't look and sound like people here!' [89] And South African critics did have something to say about the conceptualisation of this production: 'Such a bizarre, unthinking melange of styles ... serves only to raise maddening questions, both serious and facetious, in the minds of bewildered audiences ... What a waste, what a ridiculous, misconceived waste ... This is a botched, insultingly unsubtle production of an often misunderstood, marvellous play.' [90] Criticism is taken by Sher as evidence of the South African provinciality that cannot appreciate his vision; there is no indication in any of the writing he has put out about the staging of his *Titus* that he ever thought through the critiques. 'At last', he says of his first British reviews, 'a palpable sense of excitement about what we're doing. At last – the realisation of our original concept.' [91]

Given his opinion of South African culture, it is not surprising that even when they do get 'terrific reviews' from South African papers, Sher is not 'unduly excited' ('It's hard to be, when we don't know any of these critics. I mean, are they any *good* at their jobs?' [92]). Furthermore, when a review is 'very nice', 'again, we can't get over-excited. White South Africans are very free with their superlatives. They say stunning instead of good ... and call every second bottle of wine a Grand Cru' [93] (as opposed to the 'superlatives' with which the *Glasgow Herald*'s review 'glows', which make 'heartwarming stuff to read' [94]). So this undiscerning public are not qualified to comment on the production adequately, in order to like it. And they are certainly in no position, cultural or moral, to dislike it.

As much as they don't take their good South African reviews seriously, when Sher and Doran receive bad reviews, they are vitriolic. As an introduction to their reviews in the *Weekly Mail* (now the *Mail & Guardian*), an independent newspaper with the kind of Struggle credentials Sher lays claim to, Sher falls back on his authority as a translator of the South African scene: 'Many readers are increasingly irritated by its intellectual posturing.' [95] In his response to the review of Digby Ricci, who did not like the production, Sher quotes Ricci ('Nobody is demanding the crystalline voices of a Vanessa Redgrave or a John Gielgud from a local cast ... ') and then comments: 'All in the same pompous ... style – for which he can't be blamed ... Nobody is demanding the crystalline opinions of a Kenneth Tynan or a Harold Hobson from a local critic.' [96] Instead of genuinely objecting to Ricci's preference for a British mould for Shakespeare, Sher cattily endorses this preference for all things British.

Sher firmly nails his colours to the mast when he declares, 'At last, a grown-up review of what we've done.' This means not only a positive review, but a British one: 'The British *Sunday*

Times devotes a two-page spread to our production.' Sher goes on to link the *Weekly Mail's* reviewers' negative response to his production not only to their incompetence, but to their locality: 'It isn't the fault of Digby Wigby or Mark Ge-vicious that their practical experience of Shakespeare is limited (though they could be blamed for shouting their ignorance from the rooftops).' [97]

'Shakespeare will ... provide'

In its conceptualisation and the responses that were forthcoming from the South African audience, as well as in Sher's reaction to these responses, preconceived notions of the cultural worth attached to national identity constructions – 'the English'; 'the South African' – can be seen to be at work. It is these notions which informed the decision to stage a Shakespeare play in South Africa in 1995, and which subsequently informed the reasons given for this decision. That Sher and Doran thought it apposite to use *Titus* to comment on reconciliation points to their assumptions about the meaning of 'Shakespeare' as an iconic figure of universal humanity, whose lessons about life will always soothe and resolve. Doran comments: '[S]urely, to be relevant, theatre must have an umbilical connection to the lives of the people watching it. How can I provide that? I suppose the answer is that I won't. Shakespeare will.' [98] And Shakespeare's moral and cultural authority is invoked, ultimately, by the time Sher and Doran come to reflect on the process of this production and its reception, to comment not on post-apartheid South Africa, but on Sher's crisis of identity, and 'South Africa's' inadequate response to his gift of his Shakespeare-bearing self.

From the evidence of the book, including Sher's responses to the negative South African reviews, it becomes clear that Sher's experience of his time in South Africa working on a Shakespeare production was, from the beginning, filtered through a specific series of expectations. These expectations were linked to Sher's unreconstructed assumptions about the meaning of the 'South African'. Sher's assumptions about cultural meaning and value were weighted to understand the British as the preferred norm, and to find the South African refusal to submit to that norm not only disappointing, but a personal attack. The South African response is so personal because Sher is exploring aspects of his own expatriate, white, identity in choosing to stage Shakespeare in post-apartheid South Africa.

What is being staged, then, is not an engaged contribution to post-apartheid South Africa, but a drama of self, a performance of an identity crisis, against the backdrop of a particular, and tiresomely familiar, binary conception of centre and periphery, and one which in this case re-enacts Achebe's Conrad effect. Sher and Doran's responses to doing *Titus* in South Africa, as documented in *Woza Shakespeare!*, offer an example of a performance of identity through identification with a particular notion of culture – invoked by 'Shakespeare' – and, when the audience reception is unexpected, of emphatic dis-identification from the 'South African'. Ultimately, what emerges from an analysis of the writing about the production is an illustration of how the Shakespeare play becomes the thing to catch the self-fashioning of the expat, and the still-extant colonial construction of the 'African'.

This version of a coconut Shakespeare – white, indeed, on the inside, in a reductive and simplistic way – is an inheritance of the apparently universal, actually thoroughly English, colonial construction of basic humanity via, in part, a liberal version of Shakespeare's meaning. The construction of Shakespeare's meaning happens first, and in some ways most crucially, in the act of editing on which all editions of the texts depend. The next chapter will explore the editing of Shakespeare's texts for post-apartheid South African schools. It is in schools that the next generation of 'coconuts' are being formed, in part through their access to English and usually, in some form or another, then to Shakespeare. If the meaning of coconuttiness in the national imaginary is to change, so that we can own its meaning as intrinsically South African (if belonging only to an elite), then school should be a crucial place to access the actually complex history of English, and of Shakespeare.

CHAPTER 4

Begging the questions:

Producing Shakespeare for post-apartheid South African schools

Andile Mngxitama's *City Press* article 'Coconut Kids Have Lost Touch with Their Roots' was mentioned in the Introduction. It was written in 2007, presumably at least partly in response to the publication of Matlwa's *Coconut* novel in the same year. [1] As we have seen, Mngxitama characterises the young black elite of post-apartheid South Africa in the usual reductive terms of the coconut: 'One of the peculiar ... developments of post-apartheid South Africa has been the rapid emergence of influential young people who are neither black nor white.' [2] That he finds it 'peculiar' that access to privilege should equal the creation of what he calls 'an assimilated elite' suggests that Mngxitama, like others who understand coconuttiness in this wholly binary and negative way, does not know the history of education in the country. Mngxitama deplores the ways these children are educated into being 'nothing but agents of whiteness', who 'will in the end denounce their own parents as too black and backward'. They cover their 'white souls', he says, with commodified markers of superficial blackness, like 'Biko t-shirt[s], beads and seshweshwe tops'. The egregious whiteness of these coconut kids is exemplified, of course, in the English that they 'spit ... through the nose', encouraged by parents who want them to succeed in a world where only English will get you anywhere. Mngxitama is critical of young people who 'don't want to be burdened by history', worrying that '[w]ithout an appreciation of how history defines the present, one invariably ends up blaming the poor for their predicament'. He is most concerned by the intrinsic racism he sees as part and parcel of coconuttiness, and the reduction of all political values to commercial ones.

The complaints that young South Africans are tired of the burden of the past, and that neo-liberal globalised values are problematic for our emerging society, are cogent concerns, although the causes and solutions are a little more complex than blaming English and a simplified version of rich, racist 'whiteness'. What is notable in Mngxitama's article for the purposes of this book is the noting, as if new, as if uniquely post-apartheid, of a social situation which goes back to the founding of the country. I'm not suggesting that there are no differences between colonial and post-apartheid South Africa. But I am suggesting that the figure of the 'coconut', burdened with the accusations of self-hatred or cultural rejection which the assumed imperative for social advancement in a neo-colonial society apparently common-sensically ensures, is intrinsically part of what it has always meant to be a particular kind of South African. The coconut kids are not a new invention. They belong to what this country is. As such, they cannot be inauthentically African.

Their relationship to English and thence to Shakespeare comes through their access to high-quality education, a privilege most South African children cannot depend upon. As we have seen, there is a coconut Shakespeare in South African literary and cultural history, who could help to formulate new terms for identification that get beyond the toxic politics of the binary formation. But, I will argue in this chapter, examining the Shakespeare editions being specifically produced for post-apartheid schools suggests that the 'universal' Shakespeare is still very much in residence. What cultural, ideological, and identity work is being done in the name of 'Shakespeare' in South Africa today?

The meanings of Shakespeare in post-apartheid South African schools are far closer to Antony Sher's Shakespeare than to Sol Plaatje's. The meanings of Shakespeare in our schools also point to the ongoing limitations of our conceptualisations of culture. The uses of Shakespeare in our educational systems do not fulfil the potential suggested by the uses of Shakespeare in our literary history.

I would like to acknowledge at the start of this chapter that there are many dedicated English teachers who do the best work possible in egregious conditions, and that this work is indeed valuable and good. In addition, while I look critically at a range of Shakespeare editions, I am not evaluating how well these editions function in practice, as teaching tools. My critique is not one informed by education theory, or by the pressures of school classroom work, neither of which are my areas of expertise. Instead this argument is concerned with 'Shakespeare' as a cultural signifier and with how material practices contribute to the meaning of that signifier. Many of the arguments about Shakespeare's texts that circulate in the university system are difficult to import into the school classroom. The kinds of readings of Shakespeare I seek to problematise here are those that most schoolteachers currently are able to teach. The alternative possible interpretations, which I suggest are precluded by the available teaching technologies, are not currently available to most schoolteachers. The gap between the theory developed in universities and the school practices recorded in and enabled by the editions under discussion is part of the point, indeed, of writing this book. This chapter is therefore also concerned with the isolation of work conducted by academics in Shakespeare Studies from 'real-world' teaching practices, especially given that the theoretical approaches which have challenged these practices invest high stakes in them, arguing that they help to reproduce problematic social relations. [3] I seek to demonstrate that the theoretical lessons learned by Anglo-American Shakespeare Studies in the last few decades, which have come to dominate university-level Shakespeare Studies methodologies internationally, have had little effect on how Shakespeare is generally received, here (and elsewhere). This is particularly pertinent to us in South Africa in the context of ongoing debates about the role of the university in our society, and about curriculum change in the interests of transformation.

I am not arguing for the removal of Shakespeare from our curricula. Questions of relevance are red herrings, whose logic belongs to a colonial and apartheid past. All culture is relevant, and available to all of us, especially culture so invested with poetic, symbolic, and economic power. Furthermore, Shakespeare is a part of our literary history as South Africans, and so a part of our South African culture. The texts are also a part of the world culture in which we participate. Rather than arguing 'for' or 'against' Shakespeare in our schools, here I seek to explore what our technologies of learning shape as possible responses to Shakespeare and all 'he' stands for, which is constructed by and implicated in material processes. This belies the logic of a universal Shakespeare. It is especially worth talking about now, when South Africans are actively and energetically engaging with what might comprise South African culture. In our current climate, where race, nationality, class, and gender politics are all being deployed in often literal life-and-death struggles over what 'we' should be, the example of how 'Shakespeare' has been constructed becomes useful precisely because it interrupts what seems self-evident about cultural worth and moral value. Or, in the terms I have been deploying all along, Shakespeare's relation to coconuttiness can complicate what we think we know about race, language, identity, and South Africanness, if we open it up to new ways of reading. This involves drawing attention to how old ways of reading perpetuate, and what their implications might be.

Previous South African critics have tried to do something similar. Martin Orkin has argued that Shakespeare was mobilised in the name of apartheid education to naturalise and authorise state practices, and went on to assert in later work that the Shakespeare text edited for South African schools epitomised a conservative political ethos. [4] David Johnson, in *Shakespeare and South Africa* (1996), points to the historically conservative ideological and political agendas behind the presence of Shakespeare in South African curricula. Both Orkin and Johnson draw on cultural materialist and post-colonial methodologies, and related work on the development and institutionalisation of English Literature as a discipline and of the role of Shakespeare within this history. [5] I do not agree with all of their conclusions, [6] but I am convinced by the point that Shakespeare's historical incarnations help to shape what the texts can and do mean in specific societies. There is no intrinsic reason – such as a putative universal truth-value – why Shakespeare's texts should be made to speak to current South African issues outside of the logic of the colonial system which entrenched Shakespeare as the paragon of English literature and thus human expression.

'English without Shakespeare would be no English'

Nevertheless, the seemingly inexorable logic of Shakespeare's Shakespearean status as the poetic voice of the universally human relentlessly reinscribes itself despite what academics have been saying about the material history of cultural worth for decades. As I mentioned in chapter one, influential branches of tertiary Shakespeare Studies have long acknowledged that the material and political history of the entrenchment of Shakespeare is as responsible for Shakespeare's position in the world cultural market as any transcendental value 'his' texts may have. [7] Much of this work made its mark in the 1980s, and is not, by now, news.

At the same time, the dominance of what Graham Holderness has termed Bardolotrous discourse [8] remains powerfully present in secondary education systems globally, despite decades of sometimes bitter contestation at universities, also globally. Schoolteachers continue to insist on Shakespeare's universal relevance and related centrality to English Literature. [9] The curriculum adviser for English in the Western Cape, at the time, Phumla Satyo, said that when curriculum transformation was discussed in 1996, and she suggested that Shakespeare should not be compulsory on the English first-language syllabus, '99.9 [% of] teachers who responded to that said: "English without Shakespeare would be no English"' (interview, 5 October 2003). Until 2010, Shakespeare was the only dramatist mentioned by name on both first- and additional-language literature syllabi, since being made compulsory in South African schools in 1930. Shakespeare is no longer compulsory on either syllabus, and increasingly Grade 12 – or final year – teachers are preferring to set the modern drama option, since it is easier to teach and students fare better in the final exam. Some schools teach

Shakespeare in the two years preceding the final year, to first-language speakers. [10]

The move away from Shakespeare as a necessary part of an education in English is consonant with the picture of a proficiency in Shakespeare as decorative at best, presented in *Coconut*, and damaging at worst, presented in the public discourse around Thabo Mbeki post-Polokwane, as I take up in the final chapter. I have been arguing for the historical continuity and relevance of Shakespeare's relationship to the coconuts of South Africa, even as I am tracking a process which may culminate in a current commonsensical version of Shakespeare which sees 'him' as, precisely, irrelevant and outdated, belonging not even just to the 'white' part of the coconut, but to the useless decorative fluff. This is, as I have been seeking to demonstrate, an historically ill-informed and theoretically impoverished version of what Shakespeare stands for in South Africa, and of what English is to South Africans. It is also a version which is informed by some kind of common-sense awareness of the limitations of the 'universal' Shakespeare, that high-cultural icon of Englishness.

Teaching Shakespeare

Many secondary-level educational authorities still insist on Shakespeare's universal relevance, even as individual schoolteachers in Anglophone countries confirm that the actual teaching of Shakespeare is anything but the experience of seamless applicability. *Teaching Shakespeare into the Twenty-first Century* presents itself as a series of American 'success stories', [11] and a schools project in Britain, whose results were published as *Shakespeare for All in Secondary Schools*, demonstrates that British children have similar difficulty accessing the texts. [12] In South

Africa, an article entitled 'Taking the Fear out of Shakespeare' begins:

> For many teachers, the teaching of Shakespeare is a matter of laborious line-by-line translations and explanations ... this boring and cumbersome task ... often, instead of simplifying the text, ends up making it more difficult and formidable. All that the teacher succeeds in doing is displaying to the pupils how much s/he knows, or does not know, about Shakespeare. [13]

While the teaching of Shakespeare presents challenges for very many teachers, the 'problem' of Shakespeare in the South African classroom is inevitably exacerbated by also being racialised, which in part means linked to issues of access to resources. During apartheid, studies of literature in the 'black' classroom invariably engaged with the question of the problematic teaching of Shakespeare. [14] In his report on the findings of the Shakespeare Schools' Text Project in 1988, run by the Institute for the Study of English in Africa at Rhodes University, André Lemmer describes excruciating teaching methods for second-language students of Shakespeare. Partly to blame was teachers' own inadequate grasp of the linguistic and cultural history to which the texts belong. He concluded, '[W]e need to "activate" the pupils' own "schemata".' [15] Lemmer suggested the need for tailored editions to help address this problem, something the Shakespeare Schools' Text project went on to produce, resulting in versions of *Macbeth*, *Othello*, *Romeo and Juliet*, *The Merchant of Venice*, and *Julius Caesar* that were designed to address the needs of South African secondary schoolchildren and their teachers.

Published by Macmillan, these editions for schools use text from *The Complete Oxford Shakespeare*. Replete with framing and explicatory material, these editions do their utmost to speak to South African students. Historical information is dealt with in a brief section which follows the play-text, and provides a summary of the play, a paragraph on 'Who was Shakespeare?' and another on 'The Theatre in Shakespeare's Time'. Notes addressed to the teacher end each play, with suggestions on how to plan Shakespeare lessons. These editions were designed in response to problems articulated by the Shakespeare Schools' Text project, and may very well function successfully as school teaching technologies. The following analysis does not seek to deny their usefulness, especially in the adverse conditions of the classroom in the 1980s when they were first formulated. However, I do suggest that a perusal of one of the plays, reissued in 1994, shows the effects of traditional editing practices on reproducing a specific kind of Shakespeare. While the text may well function in more nuanced ways in practice than a straight analysis of its formal construction can allow for, at the least, perhaps in part because of when it was developed, this edition does not seek to offer learners different kinds of access to the Shakespeare text. Looking at the editorial work done here helps to elucidate how old interpretations of Shakespeare remain entrenched in schools.

The Macmillan *Macbeth*

The Macmillan *Macbeth* (chosen here because *Macbeth* is one of the most frequently set plays in South Africa, and very popular amongst schoolteachers [16]) begins with a page on 'How to use this book'. [17] Included amongst the instructions is the advice to '[c]oncentrate on key scenes', references to which are provided.

Thus both how and what to read is structured for the reader at the outset, towards an explicit purpose: '[Y]ou'll find that meaning and understanding grow until you can quite easily fulfil the requirements of your final exams.' The emphasis on undertaking the task of reading in order to cope with a standardised exam helps to explain this edition's high level of mediation of the play's meaning. This extends from the list of characters (organised in an implicit hierarchy, in family groupings, with Duncan, his sons, and his captain at the top, followed by Macbeth's household, and the witches second-last before the list of bit-part characters), to the subtitles given to each scene, and the summary which follows each subtitle.

Before the reader gets to these summaries, there is a page of 'Suggestions for discussions and activities' to be completed before reading each act. These include culturally loaded questions for group discussion, such as: 'Do you believe in witches? Do other people believe in them? Why?' [18] Given the frequency with which *Macbeth* is considered 'appropriate' for Africans because of its superstition and its clannishness, [19] this question would seem to be designed to encourage pupils to connect the world of the play with a particular notion of African 'tradition', presumably to point out its relevance to the South African locale. At the same time, an interpretative framework is put in place which precludes any discussion of the witches' prophecies as anything other than the traditional 'equivocation' which manipulates Macbeth into doing evil:

> Find your weekly horoscope ... Does it seem true in any way? Why? (For example, you may be a Virgo and your 'stars' might say that 'plans for the future may have to be altered to please others'. Why is this likely to be accurate?) [20]

Terry Eagleton's [21] provocative reading, that the witches are the real heroes of the play (because they deconstruct the status quo), is inconceivable here.

A moral interpretation of Macbeth's actions is sealed in the glosses and framing material: in the first scene, subtitled 'We meet the witches', the assumed community of readers is positioned as opposed to everything the witches represent: 'Fair is foul and foul is fair' is glossed as 'Things that are normally good and beautiful for us are horrible and bad for the witches. What we think is foul and nasty is wonderful in their eyes.' [22] Thus, the reading of *Macbeth* as a play about the disruption of lawful order by unconscionable ambition is entrenched. There is no possibility for alternative readings, such as Alan Sinfield's suggestion that *Macbeth* could be read in part as demonstrating the workings of state-sanctioned violence. [23]

Equally, any chance of exploring the play's gendered meanings is prevented by this edition. Act I Scene v, entitled 'Lady Macbeth finds a way', begins by summarising Lady Macbeth's response to her husband's letter, foreclosing any reading of her words or actions other than as those responsible for 'mak[ing] sure that they get the throne'. Included in the gloss on her soliloquy is the question, 'Would it be fair to say that, for Lady Macbeth, fair is foul, and foul is fair?' [24] 'Unsex me here' means 'Take away all my womanly qualities (such as tenderness, love and pity)'. [25] There is no engagement with the gendered assumptions reproduced by the editors and, presumably, meant to be taken as given in class.

Feminist-informed readings, or readings such as Eagleton's and Sinfield's, which deliberately fly in the face of traditional readings of *Macbeth*, may be inaccessible to most schoolteachers. Nevertheless, it is not inconceivable to introduce these ideas into editions produced for schools, and editors interested in doing so could find ways of including a section on theoretical thinking, as they have long included sections on thinking about production values, itself once a new approach to teaching Shakespeare texts. Provocative or different approaches at least make available the knowledge that the play has multiple possible interpretations. To close down the play's meanings is formally to reproduce the kind of limited and limiting Shakespeare against which Orkin originally protested, even if individual teachers are free to extend what the text can mean in classroom practice.

By pointing out its traditional interpretative choices, I do not mean to undermine this edition's intentions as a useful tool for a beleaguered education system, or its efficacy in the classroom. I want to attempt to improve on what editing Shakespeare makes possible, in theory, which is a starting point for practice, even if the practice is itself a complicated affair. The conservatism of this edition, given its genesis as a response to the 'problem' of Shakespeare for second- and additional-language English speakers, is especially disturbing of any easy assumptions about the rightness of Shakespeare's ongoing textual and iconic presence in the post-apartheid South African classroom.

The Maskew Miller Longman *Macbeth*

More recently, the publisher Maskew Miller Longman has produced an 'Active Shakespeare' series which seeks to provide interesting ways for students to approach the text as performance, while also specifically drawing out issues of structure, genre, and 'traditional' issues such as theme and character. Editions produced are *Hamlet, Othello, Romeo and Juliet, A Midsummer Night's Dream, Julius Caesar, Macbeth,* and *Twelfth Night.*

In its marginalia – 'Words and images', 'Tools of the trade', 'Character file', 'Producer's notebook', 'In the background', and so on – this edition of *Macbeth* [26] provides visually heteroglossic interpretative, production, and historical information. The 'Active Shakespeare' series is far less controlling of its reader, although it is in some ways structurally similar to the Macmillan series. It, too, dispenses with historical information until after the play-text itself, and it also provides other kinds of framing introductory material instead. This edition of *Macbeth*'s Act I is entitled, 'Prophecies and Plots: "All hail Macbeth, that shalt be king hereafter"'. It prefaces each act with a list of quotations to be discussed 'before you read the act', and concludes with a 'storyboard' which illustrates further quotes from the act. There is also an 'After the act' section. This is designed to reiterate plot content ('write a telegram ... to summarise the action of the scene') and to raise interpretative questions ('To what extent do you think the Weird Sisters and Lady Macbeth are responsible for Macbeth's decision to go ahead and kill the king?' – a more open-ended version of the question asked by the Macmillan edition, which implicitly connects the witches and the lady). [27]

This edition uses a range of visual and informative devices to make the play approachable. Its final section, 'A note to the user of the book', [28] emphasises the interactive elements of this text, and of Shakespeare's text as play-text. Its intentions are similar to the Macmillan series – both want to make thematic connections between the play and the lives of students; both want to avoid presenting the text as encumbered with gloss and therefore as impenetrable without expert assistance – although its realisation is more sophisticated and less regulatory. As such, in my opinion it is the better educational edition of the two.

Both editions work extremely hard to provide learners and teachers with multiple points of entry into the text. But both editions ultimately beg the questions they attempt to answer. The fact remains, the more these editions try to make Shakespeare's language and cultural context 'accessible', the more they point to the gap between the texts and the students' lives. In the teaching of Shakespeare in schools, history becomes a problem. In order to locate the plays properly and explain their linguistic and cultural references, 'background' information is necessary. This often becomes the most boring aspect of teaching the text, and many teachers advocate circumventing it as much as possible [29] – hence, presumably, the relegation of only basic contextual information to the end of the text in each series.

Shakespeare 2000: 'Modernised' *Macbeth*

The other way in which history manifests as problematic is, of course, in the difficulty of what is, for many, a complex variant of an already second or third language, although the linguistic difficulty is by no means confined to additional-language English speakers, as has been suggested above. One solution to the difficulty of the language is to 'modernise' the text, as many teachers do in their classroom practice. [30] It has also been done formally by Walter Saunders, a retired Professor of English from the University of Bophuthatswana (a former nominally independent 'homeland', created by the apartheid government; the place of his professorship is not mentioned in the publicity material for the later incarnation of these editions, although it does make use of the fact of his professorship). In the early 1990s, Saunders began working on a series of editions called 'Introducing Shakespeare', which abridged and paraphrased the canonical texts in order to overcome students' resistance caused by the experience of difficulty. [31] By 2000 this series had evolved into 'Shakespeare 2000' editions, which print the modernised version next to the 'original' text, and were being used in South

Africa and England, apparently to great acclaim from students, teachers, and academics. Promotional 'Comments on the Series' include:

> 'This is an exciting project, designed to make Shakespeare more accessible for a new generation of readers. It is greatly to be welcomed.' – Prof. Susan Bassnett, University of Warwick, U.K.

> 'Walter Saunders is doing for Shakespeare what Neville Coghill did for Chaucer in making his work live for many people who would not otherwise have been able to appreciate it.' – Lord Randolph Quirk, leading British linguist

> 'The modernised *Macbeth* enabled my students to achieve record results.' – Carol Weale, Dane Court Grammar School, Broadstairs, Kent, U.K.

> 'A lifeline to Shakespeare' – Tessa Edwards, Oakhill College, Knysna, South Africa

> 'Walter Saunders has slain the Jabberwock of incomprehension that, for so many pupils, bars the way to Shakespeare's magical world.' – Jonathan Paton, Senior Lecturer, Education Dept, University of the Witwatersrand [32]

The 'Shakespeare 2000' series was meant to accommodate readers other than those within the education system, who want to understand Shakespeare but found their experiences within the education system inadequate to the task: 'For those

Third World plebs like myself who groped and plodded through Shakespeare by candlelight and still remained mystified by the Bard's archaic language, this modernised series will come as a boon', journalist Joe Khumalo is recorded as saying in the series' promotional material. [33]

In the general introductory material, Education academic Jonathan Paton recounts some of the strategies used to 'persuade teachers, without more ado, that the answer to the problem of teaching Shakespeare is to introduce the plays in the language of today'. [34] In helping to promote the series, Paton spoke as Shakespeare:

> At educational conferences and meetings with teachers I helped Walter promote his idea by performing a short monologue ... Dressed in a costume based on the Stratford bust, I would appear as William Shakespeare, having come back to earth in modern times. Here is part of my speech:

> One of the many things that fascinated me was the changes to the English language. I began to make notes, taking down new words and expressions wherever I went ... Then one day I wandered into a theatre where, to my surprise and delight, I realised they were rehearsing one of my plays. I sat down quietly at the back to enjoy it, but the more I listened, the more I realised something wasn't right. After a while I couldn't contain myself; I jumped up and said out loud, 'But people don't speak like that anymore! What d'you think would happen in my own time, if I'd used the language of Chaucer in my plays? ... I don't know how you're going to get away with this play in

its old style ... ' ... I was thrown out of the theatre, and my notebook which I'd offered them, full of words and phrases people *do* use, was thrown out after me. So, a bit saddened, I picked up the scattered pages and continued my explorations in this brave new world – for so it still seemed to me. Then imagine my horror one day when I discovered that my plays, designed to give *pleasure*, were a compulsory form of *study* in schools, and that the captive young had to sit and listen to teachers reading my lines in dreary expressionless voices, constantly having to stop and explain ... [35]

The point is cleverly made. Allowing Shakespeare to point out 'himself' that 'his' plays were never meant to be opaque, that they are supposed to be culturally *of* the time of their performances, emphasises that what makes them great is their original immediacy and relevance. But besides the ideologically fraught issue of their greatness, what makes Shakespeare's plays Shakespeare's plays? The two editions discussed above suggest that the specificities and localities of the texts (not the generalities of human emotions, or of stories which come from, and repeat, elsewhere) require the most interventions. For many schoolchildren and teachers today, Shakespeare is the crux of 'his' own texts. What Paton's monologue elides in pointing out that Shakespeare was accessible in 'his' own time, is precisely the implications of the fact that 'he' is no longer as accessible in ours. In using the fact of Shakespeare's historically specific linguistic and cultural vocabulary to argue for the logic of updating 'his' language into our own, the very historical difference to which this situation attests is enlisted to erase its implications. The putatively ahistorical nature of Shakespeare's texts is proved by pointing to their very historical material form.

The historical meaning of, and in, the 'play in its old style' *is* the Shakespeare play. Here Paton suggests that it is possible to alter the form without affecting the meaning. Furthermore, in the image of poor Will tossed onto the South African street with 'his' rejected notebook fluttering after him is the promise that Saunders will deliver the contents of Shakespeare's notebook in his therefore 'authentic' modernisations. This authorisation is reflected on the cover, which promises 'William Shakespeare's *Macbeth* in modern English by Walter Saunders'. The author, presenting Shakespeare's texts, is Saunders. The cover graphic of Shakespeare in jeans and trainers is a visual representation of this conflation of 'old' and 'modern' into one 'authentic' textual body. The manifold ironies of Shakespeare quoting 'himself' as 'he' picks up 'his' 'scattered pages' are apposite here – following post-colonial and feminist problematisations of Miranda's description of the Milan to which she will 'return' – that is, to which she is going for the first time – and in the light of Aldous Huxley's invocation of the same phrase to describe his dystopian vision, the 'brave new world' of modern English may have a more complicated relationship with translating Shakespeare's language than Paton's sketch wants to suggest.

Different in size and layout to the previous editions discussed (the other two are A4, whereas the Shakespeare 2000 *Macbeth* is closer to an A5 pocketbook size), this 'Shakespeare 2000' text begins with a twelve-page introduction, followed by the two 'versions' of the play, and leaves other editorial paraphernalia to the Notes and Glossary which follow the main body of the texts. With the 'modernised version' running alongside the so-called original, there is less need for other kinds of explanation (although some parts of the 'translation' are less 'direct' than others: the Sergeant's denigration of Macdonwald as 'Worthy to be a rebel, for to that / The multiplying villainies of nature / Do swarm upon him' [36] is 'translated' as 'Macdonald, who so swarms / With lice and other evils he's only fit / To be a rebel'). Furthermore, a dated phrase like 'fagged out' (Sergeant: 'All uncertain it was: / The armies like two swimmers so fagged out / They cling to one another and can't budge' [37]) arguably requires as much explanation as Shakespeare's 'original', and is not in the Glossary, which contains both early modern and modern words, since 'the book is aimed at a wide variety of readers'. [38]

The so-called original comes from 'the standard texts of today', that is, those that attempt 'to arrive at what [modern editors] consider to be Shakespeare's original handwritten texts'. [39] This is a very recent edition that entirely overlooks current bibliographic work, which demonstrates that for us, there can be no such thing as 'Shakespeare's original ... texts', [40] while drawing on the reputed erudition of a Shakespeare scholar to authorise itself. Either Saunders is unaware of this recent work, or he is obscuring its conclusions in order to secure the authority of his 'translation'. Either way, the authenticating position of Shakespeare scholar is ill-invoked.

The Introduction begins with a brief summary of the play, and then a section entitled 'Macbeth and Lady Macbeth'. [41] Through this detailed explanation (which is also, of course, an interpretation), their relationship is made the entry point to the play, which then becomes about criminality and guilt, and the cost immorality exacts on love. Following historical information, there is a section on '*Macbeth*'s significance today: the play's themes', [42] which casts the play's 'More important ... significance' in 'what it says ... about ambitious politicians of all times ... [Macbeth's behaviour towards Macduff's family is] mass murder, or genocide'. [43] Shakespeare shows us ' ... the triumph of justice over tyranny'. This is a disturbingly reductive and ahistorical reading, especially for such a modern edition.

It may well be that learners make excellent use of this edition. The Shakespeare 2000 website provides testimony from learner Katherine Rorich, of the well-resourced private school Herschel in Cape Town: 'When I studied the original *Macbeth* in class for matric, [44] I found it boring, but when I read the modernised version I thoroughly enjoyed it and learnt far more about the play.' [45] The efficacy of these editions' modernisation is at least suggested by the range of positive responses, albeit their source a publicity site. However, the relief with which the modernised Shakespeare is greeted surely raises the question of why education departments continue to torture their teachers and students with the original. Paton suggests reading the modernised version first in order to understand the story and the characters, before 'tackl[ing]' the 'original'. [46] As an educational strategy this may well be a good idea; it does, however, beg the question of why a reader should tackle the original at all, once the apparently obvious logic of the universal Shakespeare is seen to conflict with the historical specificity of the texts on which it depends.

Whose Shakepeare in South African schools?

Evident in all three of these recent editions of *Macbeth*, all of which were designed for the South African classroom, is, to varying degrees, the reinscription of those aspects of 'traditional' Eng Lit teaching long problematised in the academy, including a normative political and sexual morality, an insistence on resolution, and the reinscription of authority. One question then becomes, what are the implications for post-apartheid South

African subjectivities? According to cultural materialist theory, this normative morality forges a notion of high culture which imposes a specific English identity on students of literature. [47] Similarly, this way of teaching literature educates its students into believing in, and coerces them into submitting to, the authority of the text, the literary critic, and the teacher. [48] Orkin suggests that to continue to present conservative readings of the plays is to ensure that children are taught 'the importance of preserving order' in a way which 'help[s] preserve apartheid modes of thinking'. [49]

The theoretical costs of the reinscription of a Shakespeare who is universal because 'he' can be made relevant by jettisoning what is actually Shakespearean about the texts are, at the very least, the reinscription of an ahistorical Shakespeare, and a reliance on traditional 'literary' assumptions about character that are at odds with the material conditions of early modern play production; [50] in other words, the kinds of reading of Shakespeare against which now-dominant metropolitan university criticism initially reacted. This suggests that work done in universities in the past few decades has had little effect on the teaching of Shakespeare in schools, beyond disseminating an awareness that Shakespeare has become contested territory. In South African terms, this awareness is often used defensively, in reaction to what is assumed to be an 'Africanist' and thus an anti-'European' (in other words, white) position.

The emotional investment in 'Shakespeare' made by members of an Anglophone society is not to be underestimated. Karen Cunningham has shown that what is at stake when Shakespeare is perceived to be under threat is 'the order and rationality of society: to change Shakespeare's position is to act irrationally and to precipitate anarchy'. [51] Cunningham's context is American; a similar alarmed reaction occurred in South Africa in 2001 when a group of teachers tried to get some of the plays banned, as mentioned in chapter one. As in Cunningham's example, the debate was picked up by the media in highly specific ways. The tone of the reportage pointed to what 'Shakespeare's' presence in South African syllabi is seen to be protecting or ensuring, and to the fears of displacement under a post-apartheid dispensation felt by those who identify with this 'Shakespeare'. [52]

Of course, Shakespeare's texts and cultural capital have been owned and enjoyed by many South Africans, regardless of 'race'. We have seen that Shakespeare's texts and iconic status played a part in anti-colonial and anti-apartheid writing in English in the region. This South African appropriation of Shakespeare, however, is absent from post-apartheid school syllabi.

The Wits Schools Shakespeare's *Macbeth*

Most recently, there has been an attempt to connect Shakespeare's *Macbeth* to the specifically South African milieu. The Wits Schools Shakespeare's *Macbeth*, published by Nasou Via Afrika in 2007, tries to 'connect Shakespeare's plays with the experience of living in South Africa today'. [53] The editors are careful to point out that the play's meaning operates, separately, in relation to its medieval setting, its early modern time of composition, and its readers' own era (the label 'postmodernity' is absent, and while this is perhaps understandable in a schools' text, a discussion of its meaning could have productively opened ways into deconstructing assumptions about the Shakespeare text at hand). The editors thus acknowledge the gap between the lives of today's South African students and the play-text, unlike the previous editions put together for our schools. The latter, I have been suggesting, inadvertently emphasise, even as they disavow, this gap, by insisting on Shakespeare's universal relevance. The Wits editors want 'to stimulate you to read works of African literature that have interesting connections with the play. In this way, Shakespeare becomes a means of introducing you, as South Africans, to your own literary heritage.' [54] Accordingly, the edition ends each act with an 'Africa Writes' section, which introduces the reader to an African writer and, usually, one of his texts in some detail. The writers are all men, and they are not all South African: Achebe and Soyinka feature. [55] The silent work of canon construction and the assumptions about African Literature as a genre that are at play here bear noting.

There is potential for allowing the Shakespeare text to open up genuine connections between itself and post-apartheid South Africa, in alternative ways of editing and teaching Shakespeare. However, much as it tries to execute this programme, the Wits Schools Shakespeare edition of *Macbeth* fails. All it succeeds in doing is once again reiterating how much Shakespeare belongs in the first instance to 'his' own time. I am not suggesting that Shakespeare's texts are not 'relevant' to South Africans. Shakespeare is as relevant to South Africa as 'he' is anywhere, and as all literature is to all humans. But when we try to invoke relevance by relying on aspects of the text that we lift out of their context, we end up emphasising precisely the ways 'his' texts do *not* specifically relate to South Africans.

The Wits *Macbeth* fails because, despite its initial acknowledgement of the different embedded contexts of the text, it opts to make the links between *Macbeth* and South Africans' 'own literary heritage' by drawing out putatively universal themes. So, as an example, a brief comment on what this edition does with the most well-known text of African Literature, *Things Fall Apart*: students are instructed to '[r]ead the following commentary on the novel ... and then discuss the commentary using the questions below'. The commentary focuses on Okonkwo's murder of Ikemefuna.

> [A]s in *Macbeth*, the sacrifice of one human being in order for others to fulfil their personal desires has a disturbing effect on us. As we know, Macbeth and Lady Macbeth murder King Duncan of Scotland with the express purpose of helping Macbeth to ... become king. On the other hand ... Okonkwo ... kills an unsuspecting boy ... so that calm and prosperity will be restored to the village ...
>
> Of particular note is that in both *Macbeth* and *Things Fall Apart* the victims had absolute trust in their murderers ... It is this betrayal of trust that places the two books side by side in emotional and artistic equilibrium. [56]

This creative link is developed further in a couple of questions rich in comparative potential, if a little repetitive:

> Okonkwo and Macbeth are both described as tragic heroes. In what way is this true?
>
> Compare and contrast Okonkwo and Macbeth. [57]

Such connections are interesting and productive in themselves. However, they also emphasise the arbitrary nature of this connection between *Macbeth* and *Things Fall Apart*. One could just as well connect Shakespeare's play to any literary work with a male anti-hero. There is nothing specifically Shakespearean about betrayal, and using a human experience to link *Macbeth* to an African text risks once again privileging the Shakespearean signifier as the universally human, making the African expression 'as good as' or 'like' the Shakespearean. [58] Of course, much depends on how this edition is used in individual classrooms, because the potential of diffusing the investment in Shakespeare's emotional and moral authority by pointing out that it exists in Achebe too, is also enabled. Given the tireless reinscription of the discourse of the universal Shakespeare in our schools and in the texts developed for them, however, it seems at least likely that this edition, contrary to its intentions, could be used not to enrich the relationship between Shakespeare and South African or African texts, but to simplify and structure it along traditional, neo-colonial lines. It is a great pity that this edition did not take the opportunity to reflect in more careful nuance and detail on the operations of material history it gestures towards in its opening delineation of the play's three levels of meaning. Indeed, on this note it is worth mentioning that the edition begins with a misrepresentation of *Macbeth's* materiality: 'Shakespeare divided the play into acts and scenes' is the opening line of the first section following the Preface. [59]

The questions our schools' Shakespeare begs of us

A range of editions of *Macbeth* developed for the South African classroom presents a picture which begs a number of questions. The problems of historical difference suggest the illogicality of insisting on Shakespeare's 'universal applicability' or 'relevance' to students on the basis of what 'he' teaches about universal humanity. The fact of the reinscription of more 'traditional' literary critical elements in the Shakespeare currently produced for schools through the editions tailor-made for them beg other questions about the relationship between schools as institutions that police civil subjects, Shakespeare as a cultural icon, and the role of universities in both of these, in the wider social context which exists outside of their 'ivory tower' walls. How much does Shakespeare really matter in post-apartheid South African culture, if an outdated version is in circulation within a society that seems to be very busily working through its complex definitions of 'culture'? Accordingly, what role, if any, should Shakespeare be assured in post-apartheid South Africa? In the context of a struggling and under-resourced education system, whose Shakespeare has the right to claim this role? If teachers are underqualified to teach the university's Shakespeare, how important is it that we insist that they address this situation? What does it mean for cultural work done in our universities? South African schoolteachers work in increasingly deteriorating conditions, with little support in the area of teacher training, amongst other areas. To teach otherwise than the way enabled by the editions discussed here would take a sustained engagement between the national Education Department, trainers of teachers, and tertiary Shakespeare scholars. However well-intentioned any of these institutions might be, very few of us have the time to talk to one another or do what we do differently.

Our post-apartheid Shakespeare raises questions about how much university theories really matter, and about what Shakespeare is actually doing in South Africa. The remaining chapters of this book provide a few answers to this last question, at least. In the last chapter, Matlwa's Shakespeare comes into focus in the context provided here, and suggests that at the moment Shakespeare is standing for the worst kind of coconuttiness, despite our much more interesting history with him. In the next chapter, I explore how Shakespeare's relation to the African Renaissance comes via the role of Eng Lit in the development of the intellectual resources required to construct a Renaissance of any sort in our post-colonial locale.

CHAPTER 5

English and the African Renaissance

Reporting on his expulsion from the presidency in 2008, the *Christian Science Monitor* headed the story of Mbeki's downfall, 'Thabo Mbeki: The Fall of Africa's Shakespearean Figure'. [1] Scott Baldauf reports in terms that will become more familiar to us in the next chapter: Mbeki's intelligence, which went together with his aloofness, is contrasted to Zuma's 'populism'. Not surprisingly, Mbeki's intelligence and aloofness are both associated with Shakespeare, here and elsewhere. What is notable here is that, just as Can Themba and Bloke Modisane explicitly do, and as critics have done with Plaatje, Mbeki self-identifies as a Shakespearean tragic hero. Interviewing his biographer, Mark Gevisser, Baldauf writes:

> Mark Gevisser reveals that Mbeki, as a young economics student at the Lenin Institute in Moscow in 1969, closely identified with the tragic Shakespearean character, Coriolanus. Mbeki saw Coriolanus as a revolutionary role model who was prepared to go to war with his own people to defend the nation's principles. In the end, Coriolanus is exiled because of his unwillingness to publicly parade after returning from a successful campaign.

> Mr. Gevisser suggested that Mbeki saw his own
> future in Coriolanus. 'The person who does good,
> and does it honestly, must expect to be overpowered
> by forces of evil,' he told Gevisser during a 1999
> interview. 'But it would be incorrect not to do good
> just because you know death is coming.'

The article ends on this note, a wholly sympathetic one, which
allows Mbeki his identification and his self-expression as a
great, if tragically wronged, character. He has been much less
sympathetically treated in the media, specifically with regard
to his penchant for Shakespeare. Mbeki's association with
Shakespeare and its meaning in the popular imagination will be
treated in more detail in the following chapter. In this chapter
I look in some detail at how the coconut president's notion of
the African Renaissance encodes the very revised meaning of
coconuttiness I have been offering. It is no coincidence that it
took a coconut to activate the notion, given its links to the idea
of Renaissance upon which Shakespeare's popular reputation
to some extent depends, and to the role of English Literature in
developing this idea of Renaissance. Mbeki's African Renaissance
belongs to the South Africa of Plaatje and Themba. It is indeed
tragic, in the Aristotelian sense that complicity is a necessary
ingredient, that the coconuttiness Mbeki has come to stand for
entails the signification of Shakespeare as something which bears
very little relevance to 'Africa'. If Mbeki's African Renaissance
was meant to reinvigorate 'Africa', in the end it seemed to prove
its own irrelevance because of its political associations. But, as I
will argue here, even more ironically, the notion of the African
Renaissance itself stands for the work of coconuttiness in ways its
proponents consistently denied.

Thabo Mbeki's Renaissance

The African Renaissance, like the Rainbow Nation, was, under Mbeki, a catchphrase for the 'new' South Africa that, despite the important project it attempted to enable, ran the risk of being emptied of real content by party-political sloganeering, commodification, and the problems of reification that informed its vocabulary. There are many tensions implicit in the concept; it continually pulls against itself, not least by virtue of its name, which traces a hybrid reality in the service of promoting an idealised, putatively pure 'African' identity. What the African Renaissance attempted to offer to an 'Africanisation' of South Africa, and indeed the world, was premised in part on the traditional subject of English Literature, according to the ways in which both constructs – the African Renaissance; English Literature – mean in relation to each other.

The term 'African Renaissance' appeared as early as 1969, but the notion of an African Renaissance led by South Africa first began to be developed by Thabo Mbeki in a speech in the United States in 1997. [2] The notion of an African Renaissance works metaphorically, and to great effect. As such it has inspired hagiographic writing exalting its premises and promises, and sometimes discussing what should constitute its strategy. Mbeki set in motion an idea of great emotional potency. This is intentional; he declared that the African Renaissance is 'our rediscovery of our soul'. [3] The valency of this idea is clear in the eagerness with which the hopes of a new dawn for Africa and Africans have been enumerated:

> The *raison d'être* for a renaissance in the African continent is the need to empower African peoples to deliver themselves from the legacy of colonialism

and neo-colonialism and to situate themselves on
the global stage as equal and respected contributors
to as well as beneficiaries of all the achievements of
human civilization. [4]

Peter Vale and Sipho Maseko detailed the 'emancipatory potential
which the idea of an African Renaissance offers the continent's
people', [5] and Chris Landsberg and Francis Kornegay emphasised
the African Renaissance's refusal of 'Afro-pessimis[m]; it
counters racist condemnations of inevitable African failure'. [6] The
African Renaissance promised to 'build a ... new African world ...
of democracy, peace and stability, sustainable development and
a better life for the people', according to Mbeki, in his 'Prologue'
to the conference proceedings of the 1998 African Renaissance
conference. [7] The psychological as well as political necessity of
such long-denied grace is evident in the alacrity with which the
felicitous rhetoric of the African Renaissance was propagated.

In the context of colonial history's constructions of Africa and
Africans, the insistence that 'Africa' cannot rely for solutions on
those who exploited and oppressed the continent and its peoples [8]
was significant in terms of the Mbeki administration's plans
for South Africa's position in continental and global political
and fiscal economies, and necessary for the development of an
empowered identity politics. That the African Renaissance proved
threatening to some white South Africans [9] further suggests
that the concept speaks to issues of identity, and of access to
resources – and that a link between the two was perceived by a
constituency accustomed to legitimising its monopolisation of
resources by mobilising a supremacist identity politics. Despite
some careful strategising to move the concept away from
exclusionary racialised discourse, [10] the concept's affective power
comes from an ability to speak to 'a consciousness of the pain and

humiliation of African people in a continent, and world, which remains entirely dominated by the cultural values of people who are not black'. [11] In other words, the second half of the phrase relies on the first. Renaissance is necessary because of what being African has been made to mean, because of histories of racialised oppression. Renaissance, in this context, cannot avoid meaning in relation to the category 'black'. [12] If racism were not a global mobilising structural force, there would be no need for a specifically African Renaissance.

The potential of the discourse to engage meaningfully with histories of oppression is mitigated by the sloganeering that has seized upon its affective power. Nevertheless, in what it offers to identity politics at the very least, the African Renaissance was more than merely a moment of political opportunism. Why? What informed and enabled the emotion which set the concept in motion? I will suggest it is the idea of a Renaissance (centrally informed by the work of Shakespeare) as developed by English Literature, and given affective valency by the position of English. In order to explicate this idea, I turn now to an investigation of the underlying metaphor. The qualifier 'African' points to another, earlier, Renaissance, and relies on it.

The European and African Renaissances

The hopes of the African Renaissance, premised as they were on a particular notion of the 'original', European Renaissance, wreak havoc with historical logic. Central to this hopeful project, which looked forward to a glorious future, was the notion of the recovery of histories that have been overlooked, denied, or lost. [13] In this way the primary connection with the notion of

'Renaissance' is established. However, the African Renaissance is a concerted effort, which its model was not. This gives rise to a conceptual disjuncture that is sometimes overlooked in the name of a project of renewal that is taking place in a very different context. A number of problematic parallels result. Thus, 'Europe [embarked] ... on a campaign to reclaim and revamp [itself]', [14] a project which, it is proposed, 'Africa' should learn from. [15] The power of agency is devolved onto continents in a way which is important in the context of the inheritances of colonialism and their implications for racialised identities, but which threatens to undermine the ontological basis of the project, since the historical connections that are meant to legitimate the idea of an African Renaissance are in fact inaccurate.

Applied across the board regardless of (perhaps most importantly) class politics, this European Renaissance is seen to have been planned by a subjectless power: 'the European Renaissance ... was created as a method to revamp the morale and objectives of Europe and its constituents'. [16] Medieval Europe is cast 'like Africa' as unstable, disease-ridden, in crisis, a situation to which a response was required: 'the warning was clear for humanity to seek knowledge and to cease bickering'; 'the European Renaissance was an answer ... [to] crises'. [17] Mahmood Mamdani sees the African Renaissance as a child of pan-Africanism, 'Africa's attempt to go beyond its Dark Ages ... did not the European Renaissance also aim to go beyond its Dark Ages, its Middle Ages, by reaching back into a dim past ... ?' [18] The European Renaissance is continually cast as a movement akin to the politicised, conscientising nature of pan-Africanism. [19] This putative coordinated continental recognition and management of crisis is anachronistically linked to a unified programme of colonial expansionism: 'the European Renaissance was not simply the freedom of spirit and body for the European men, but a new freedom to destroy freedom for the rest of humanity'; [20] 'for these objectives [of the Renaissance] to be realised, as far as Europeans were concerned, they had to conquer Africa, its indigenous peoples and their cultures'. [21] It is important to point out the ideological links between the period's burgeoning European territorial expansion, the development of nation-states and the nationalism that came with them, the advent of slavery, the invocation of an older discourse of racial difference, and the development of a new, increasingly racist, vocabulary as a result of all these forces. [22] The behaviour of societies that would eventually become the perpetrators of high colonialism does need to be accounted for in these terms. [23] However, it is patently implausible to suggest that a process, identified and named after the fact, which spanned at least two centuries (the exact dating of the 'Renaissance' is in debate) and which developed unevenly in various countries and cultures, was preplanned and coordinated, especially by a continent (standing for, metonymically, a homogenised 'European' consciousness). The parallels on which the African Renaissance has been built, in the name of historical veracity and concomitant factual legitimacy, collapse under scrutiny.

The informing drive of the African Renaissance is not, then, historical accuracy. Rather, as I have suggested, it is a psychological imperative which carries powerful identity-political implications. And as such, it is not as different from the European Renaissance as the discussion above suggests. The concept of Renaissance – European or African – is firmly presentist, and the magnificent ideological artefact erected upon its beams is composed of the idealism, emotion, and aspiration of its builders, not of the experiences or identities of those who lived in the time upon which the apparently rebirthed present is modelled. The European Renaissance is as much a fiction, a response to an inadequate present, as its younger sibling, the African Renaissance, whose proponents were seeking historical role models.

What makes a Renaissance?

The designation of the European 'Renaissance' as a discrete period is not an ideologically neutral activity. As the geographical metaphors of which much current literary theory makes use suggest – terrain is mapped, areas are explored, territory is staked, boundaries are drawn – an act of colonisation of the past takes place which is a process of simultaneous knowing and creating. [24] The term 'Renaissance' developed as a period marker in the nineteenth century. Critical consensus is that Jacob Burckhardt 'invented' the Renaissance in 1860, with the publication of his *The Civilization of the Renaissance in Italy*. [25] Hayden White suggests that Burckhardt should be read as a social scientist, not as an historian. [26] White points to the constitutive quality of his writing, making the larger point that the discourses in which history is inscribed constitute the object of study itself. Burckhardt envisioned the Italian Renaissance as the product of an ideal society, perfectly able to accommodate each individual subject, resulting in a dominating zeitgeist: 'The Italians of the fourteenth century knew little of false modesty or of hypocrisy in any shape; not one of them was afraid of singularity, of being and seeming unlike his neighbours'; [27] accordingly, it was the 'genius of the Italian people' together with the 'revival of antiquity' which 'achieved the conquest of the western world', [28] a nineteenth-century expansionist ideal. This is a clear example of 'the ineluctably interpretative element in every historical narrative worthy of the name'. [29] The resulting definition of 'Renaissance' produces a nostalgic version of the past that maps the aspirations (sometimes cast as elegies) of the present. It is not surprising, then, that Vusi Mavimbela, one of the architects of Mbeki's vision, saw the idea of a Renaissance as encoding 'a higher level of human existence'. [30]

In the light of this notion of elevated human experience, the term 'Renaissance' is implicitly a valorisation of high culture. [31] There is also, by now, a (related) commodity value to the term, as the signifier of cultural worth has been used by advertising industries. [32] Of course, the poster child of the Renaissance for Eng Lit is Shakespeare, whose social, cultural, and economic value is clear in the industries that have sprung up around him: publishing, educational, theatre, film, and, indeed, advertising.

The connection between the generation of capital and a culture to which access is limited by education suggests one of the ways in which the African Renaissance has the potential, despite its rhetoric of mass renewal, to serve an elite. [33] The African Renaissance, in its economic incarnation, was working towards inserting South Africa and Africa into a globalised arena, and as such, its proponents can be accused of seeking to entrench and profit from globally increasing material disparities even as (in spirit) the African Renaissance sought to address global imbalances. Its ideological content becomes available to a ruling elite in search of an 'election platform'. [34] At the least, a notion of culture inflected with the elitist valuation of a European high culture was invoked in the name of an essentialised and idealised pre-colonial African unity.

Despite this reliance on the associations with European high culture, an understanding of the African Renaissance as offering the opportunity for a restoration of Africanness is often predicated on a binary positioning of 'European' and 'African'. This position depends on viewing culture as an object (instead of as a practice), which can be contained and purified. [35] The invocation of a premodern homogenised Africanness mimics certain colonial constructions of 'tribal' identity, and denies the changes that African cultures, like all cultures, have undergone in time. [36] Indeed, '[t]he term *Renaissance* implicitly calls for a perception of historical rupture (in order to be reborn, a culture must previously have died)'. [37] One implication is that the definition of culture this assumes contradicts the cultural coconuttiness I have been suggesting characterises elite South African identities since the very beginning of this nation's formation. Even as the term 'African Renaissance' invokes cultural purity and control, it arises from a history of cultural mixing and unexpected response.

In its adjective-noun combination and the ideologically overdetermined content each term is called upon to signify, then, the African Renaissance pulls in two directions. In the terms of its project, too, it contains within itself two conceptualisations that exist in tension. Tom Lodge has pointed out that the African Renaissance is simultaneously composed of a vision of modernity, 'something that will be brought about by means of fibre-optic cables, liberal democracy and market economies', and of an invocation of what it denotes as 'traditional values': 'African communities succeed in reconstructing themselves around ... the values and relationships that characterised pre-colonial institutions.' [38]

For Vale and Maseko, the two discourses encoded in the African Renaissance are what they call 'globalist' (Lodge's 'modernity') and 'Africanist' (Lodge's 'traditional values'). The globalist discourse draws its momentum from the 'meta-narrative of globalisation' [39] and its logic is economic. The globalist element of the African Renaissance envisages South Africa as the leader of an economic revolution that would establish the African equivalent of 'the Asian Tigers' (their analysis was written in 1998, before the collapse of the Asian economies). In this vision, South Africa acts as the 'agent ... of globalisation' on the continent, and is rewarded financially as a result. Vale and Maseko point out that 'this is a northern understanding of development and progress'. [40] Once again, the tension in the African Renaissance, as a programme of African reification reliant in its very conceptualisation on the influences and effects of European colonialism, comes to the fore, this time in the economic aspect of the programme. It is also clear how the economic arm of the African Renaissance belongs firmly to the pressures of modernity as they have been responded to by the Englished, upwardly mobile elite from Plaatje onwards.

What Vale and Maseko designate as the 'Africanist' component of the African Renaissance is concerned with the development of a positive identity position for Africans, and resists the positioning of Africa as a market for the North. [41] As they describe it, there is a conflict between the globalist and the Africanist imperatives – between the imperatives of economic globalisation which would benefit an elite at the expense of the majority (and which is modelled on the needs of the economies of the dominant North), and those of a post-colonial identity politics which draws on solidarity and a shared positioning based on racialisation. [42] Rather, as I am suggesting, the African Renaissance can be read as the sign of a coconuttiness which is neither a nefarious tool of the colonising 'West', nor the putatively authentic voice of 'black Africa'. Instead, it instantiates another, messier, much more interesting and difficult history, which is a productive part of what it means to be South African.

Mbeki's adviser Mavimbela was as aware of cultural history as he was of the globalised context in which the 'new' South Africa was emerging. [43] He defined globalisation as a 'miracle' that 'has offered hope to the people of Africa that economic development can be rapid'. [44] Thus, for Mavimbela the African Renaissance could be successful only if it engaged with, in order to profit from, globalisation.[45] Mavimbela's vision of the European Renaissance as a model for an African counterpart saw it as reliant on an emerging economic elite (thus endorsing the charge that 'the idea of the African Renaissance is rooted in the necessity to develop and sustain an African middle class', [46] a charge which is speaking to the history of coconuttiness upon which the African Renaissance as a concept depends). Accordingly, a Renaissance depends on the annexation (through colonial or other means) of foreign markets; he draws a parallel between our current context of 'globalisation' and the 'proliferation in sea trade' of the fifteenth and sixteenth centuries. [47] This conceptualisation of the 'first' Renaissance thus correlates with a particular economic conceptualisation of the present, and, more importantly, with a set of neo-colonial cultural, economic, and political aspirations for South Africa.

What makes an African Renaissance?

Following then-Education Minister Sibusisu Bengu's contribution to the 1998 African Renaissance conference, Dalamba stated that 'culture and education need to be addressed in ways that reaffirm African values, African identity and cultural practices as they relate to the learning and teaching process and an African-based discourse'. [48] Leaving aside the obvious questions – what are 'African values ... identity ... cultural practices ... discourse[s]' in the hybrid, creole, transcultural zone that is neo-colonial, neo-apartheid South Africa in a globalising world? – I would like to ask: how, in the terms of the African Renaissance, whose affective and ideological content is enabled by Eng Lit as an institutionalised field of study and shaped by its construction of what constitutes a Renaissance, is this possible?

From its inception as a formal discipline, a normative model of subjectivity has informed Eng Lit. This model has developed within Eng Lit's location in institutions, and in its overt goals of moral and spiritual – often under the banner of 'cultural' – education. The spread of Eng Lit is one of the signs of a transnational globalisation enabled by colonialism, but is also paradoxically haunted by a nationalist (originally implicated in a colonialist) mandate. English departments now see themselves as heteroglossic centres, teaching texts from a range of literatures in English, while remaining reliant for their disciplinary definition on a specific national history. Even works that fit within the post-colonial category 'Literatures in English' take their definitional starting point from national identities, while their presence in English departments speaks for an international subject identity. [49] The revised Eng Lit, in other words, is simultaneously global and reliant on national specificity.

For Apollo Amoko, the imperative is to de-link the study of English literature from the weight of English history, an undertaking which has profound implications for the traditional canon, to which the Renaissance is central. [50] By insisting on the neo-colonial implications of the status quo within the subject, Amoko's project points to the ways in which the intention to acknowledge difference can, despite itself, entrench an unspoken normativity.

Eng Lit – even a revised Eng Lit, which still draws its institutional validity from its original incarnation – retains its Englishness in the context of a self-consciously globalised identity which comprises other nations' writing in English (the results of colonial histories). The Renaissance retains commonsensical value because of Eng Lit's global positioning and concomitant paradoxical nature. Eng Lit disseminates and authorises this high-cultural notion, with its availability as receptacle of the aspirations of the present cast into an idealised past. Consequently, the African Renaissance's economic programme is authorised by the emotional content of the concept, and both are generated by the international context in which it was developed, and to which it is a response.

The construction within Eng Lit of the English Renaissance as a golden age may, Arthur Kinney suggests, 'be viewed as a culture protesting too much'. Following Don E. Wayne, Kinney offers a view of the idealised invocation of the past – 'tradition' – which is apposite both to what the Renaissance as a period has been to Eng Lit, and to what it is being made to stand for in the development of the concept of an African Renaissance:

> [T]radition is invoked most often in order to preserve a static image of culture. Such an image has the power of eliciting from us a strong emotional commitment because it fulfills, however temporarily, our desire to escape that palpable sense of discontinuity which has marked our social and personal experience for more than a century. [51]

This assertion about the role of tradition, and traditional (high) culture, in Eng Lit is not new. What I am suggesting is that the same structures should be seen at work in the concept of the African Renaissance. Indeed, the African Renaissance draws its validatory or legitimising meaning from the same structures of thought (about culture, about value, about the past and the present) that enabled traditional Eng Lit to mean what it did. And the notion of a golden age of literary Renaissance for English is central to this meaning.

Not coincidentally, then, both Eng Lit and the African Renaissance are described as humanising by their proponents. One elaboration of the ethical potential of the African Renaissance sees it as capable of launching a global anti-racist movement: 'this renaissance should empower [the continent] to help the world rediscover the oneness of the human race'. [52] Echoing similar invocations about Eng Lit's developmental and humanist potential that were made during the course of high colonialism and continued, in different forms, into the first half of the twentieth century (and which in part gave rise to the revisionism noted by Greenblatt and Gunn [53]), Mbeki called on the African Renaissance to initiate global moral renewal, 'in order to build a planetary civilization instead of sinking down to barbarism'. [54] This vision, like the vision of the African Renaissance itself, drew on a model of 'civilisation' and a concomitant notion of universal human progress which has been integral to the development of Western culture (including colonialism) for at least the last 300 years – although the extent, emergence, definition, and role of modern Western subjectivity (of modernity, in other words) is in ongoing debate. [55]

It is within this colonial model of 'civilisation' that Eng Lit developed as a formalised field in South Africa, amongst other places. [56] It is partly as a result of the cultural component of colonialism, which has shaded into neo-colonialism, which is in turn imbricated in globalisation, that Eng Lit acquired its potency, its cultural commodity value. Because Eng Lit is what it is, the African Renaissance makes sense.

Thus Mbeki was characterised as a 'renaissance man'; [57] perhaps his double-articulation as an Africanist committed to globalisation [58] was the neo-colonial, post-apartheid embodiment

of the concept. The highly metaphorical and poetic language
of Mbeki's elaboration of the African Renaissance [59] displayed
an education in literary English. Indeed, Mbeki's literary
proficiency, while it still had purchase, was partly responsible
for the successful packaging of the promises of African renewal
expressed in the metaphor of Renaissance:

> If these circumstances [those of newly post-apartheid
> South Africa] made the notion of an African
> Renaissance propitious within South Africa, it was
> the lyrical appeal of Mbeki's imagery which turned
> the obvious, the commonsensical, into a tryst with
> history .[60]

An African Renaissance in English

English has an ambivalent history in South Africa. In part a
tool of a colonial education system, it also became available to
some South African writers in English as a means of forging
identities in opposition to apartheid constructions. It has always
been a language of class and political power, 'centrally implicated
in processes of social power in South Africa', [61] as I have been
arguing. The African Renaissance's reliance on Eng Lit, in
the name of a project of African reclamation, thus illustrates
the Gordian knot of colonial histories of oppression and the
colonised's concomitant appropriation and transformation of
elements of these experiences, in the current context of global
power relations in which English is profoundly implicated. That
the elite South African is in some sense an English subject, that is
to say, a subject of English, is encoded in the fact that the moniker

'African Renaissance' makes the kind of sense that it does. The African Renaissance, even as it was an attempt to create a counter-discourse, is part of what De Kock calls the 'social textualisation' that English provided, 'a narrative and a representation of the world'. [62] The connection between what the Renaissance means in South Africa, and the African Renaissance, runs through Eng Lit, which made available a particular notion of Renaissance to the African subjects it has in part (in)formed. [63]

Perhaps the greatest crux in the concept of the African Renaissance, then, is not the apparent contradiction of its very naming, which suggests that an idealised African culture can best be conceptualised by the model of European history, even as the concept that is being named bespeaks an awareness of the colonisation of African minds, in part by European models of history, in part by other European cultural narratives. It is not that the African Renaissance sought to authorise itself by invoking an apparent historical truth – the success of the European Renaissance – whose connections reveal themselves as anachronistic and inaccurate. It is not that this authority is dependent on a hierarchical notion of high culture, and yet said it wanted to speak for the good of 'the people'. Rather, it is that in attempting to engage with the positioning of Africa in the global imaginary, in embarking on what is an important empowerment project, the proponents of an African Renaissance reveal that their thinking is embedded in, and shaped by, the complex discursive and institutional field that is Eng Lit.

This is not to suggest that Eng Lit is the only cultural influence informing the African Renaissance; indeed, pan-Africanism is another influence, as I have mentioned above. A pan-African communication, however, is likely to take place in a language originally imported by colonialism. The extensive presence in Africa, and globally, of the English language cannot be separated from the cultural implications and educational programmes of British colonialism, of which Eng Lit was a part. It is precisely the global networks of power, politics, and economics into which the concept of the African Renaissance has to enter, and the inevitable dominance of an elite which results, that make the African Renaissance and the institution of English Literature co-dependent.

The psychological work done by the concept of the African Renaissance reveals even more complex truths about what it means to be a South African of a specific class. We have seen in earlier chapters how writers in English made use of Shakespeare as the embodiment of an education in a cultural tradition that empowered them even as it shaped them. The concept of the African Renaissance can be read for more information about this ambivalent process of subject-formation by, in, and through English.

Mbeki's African Renaissance has since fallen out of favour, along with the man himself. Significantly, his unpopularity became encapsulated in his relationship with Shakespeare, which was returned firmly to the Western half of an old colonial binary. The African subject of English, and the Shakespeare that stands (in) for it, is currently rather ambivalently, perhaps enviously, certainly suspiciously, viewed as not properly part of what South Africa should be.

CHAPTER 6

Shakespeare and the coconuts

As this book has hoped to demonstrate, South Africa has a rich Shakespearean literary and political history. Important writers and thinkers have displayed, and oftentimes clearly experienced, intellectual and emotional connections to, especially, the plays. Since the days of the mission schools in colonial southern Africa, Shakespeare has been a signifier of education, civility, and erudition, as well as a vehicle for the expression of strong feelings. Encounters with the Shakespeare text have shaped hopes, allowed for public self-fashioning, and have influenced more intimate subjectivities as writers and scholars of a particular class stratification were educated in English Literature. These men (and they were mostly men) could be seen as early versions of coconuts. As such, they help us to think through the idea of the coconut and what it stands for (a proficiency in English, economic mobility, and class privilege) as an important component of South African social history. If we accept this, we also have to challenge the additional meaning of the coconut: the inauthentically black black person. Looking at Shakespeare in South African literary history is one way to look afresh at our cultural politics, particularly in the current context where racial identities are being hardened and simplified.

Perhaps as part of this movement away from complexity and towards a simplified and impoverished version of identity, something has changed in what Shakespeare enables today. If Shakespeare used to be part of a marker of class and social mobility located in the terms of a discourse of progress and modernity, knowledge of Shakespeare now comprises a much more publicly ambivalent display. Shakespeare once had a particular currency, acquired personally but activated publicly, which 'he' appears to be losing. This chapter describes the change in more detail.

I have been arguing that key individual examples of the role Shakespeare has played in South Africa demonstrate two things. English and Englishness can be markers and tools of Africanness. At the same time, the 'universal' Shakespeare anxiously seeks to justify Shakespeare in South Africa through recourse to 'his' apparently generally human meanings, deploying the discourse of relevance along the way. Both of these meanings are colonial products. But their effects are very different from each other.

Why is Shakespeare becoming more and more like that English guy whose face dominates the second picture above, the picture of the high-cultural Pom who knows very little, and cares even less, about something called Africa whose meaning is assumed to be obvious, and obviously separate from what 'he' means? I think it may be because, in the face of ongoing socio-economic power differentials which operate along raced and classed axes, the logic of a binary structure of identity continues to inform an experience of Shakespeare in South Africa long after our own cultural artefacts reveal that binary models are an artificial and inadequate way to understand how people live, including how they live with Shakespeare. As Antony Sher's Shakespeare shows us, a binary experience of the world is still very much in operation despite a by now clear theoretical understanding that things actually work in more complicated ways. There is another crucial way in which binaries still have power to determine people's experiences here. In South Africa today, material conditions continue to worsen, and they do so mostly along inherited lines: most of the poorest people are black, and many of the country's resources, including, crucially, land, are still visibly in the hands of white people. While the actual workings of blackness and whiteness reveal them to be invested constructs that co-constitute, as indeed the history of Shakespeare in the lives and works of our writers makes clear, it isn't surprising that the lived experience of many South Africans is still that they are self-evident absolutes.

The problem with coconuts

Recent local responses to the idea of Shakespeare, and of what a deeply personal familiarity with Shakespeare might mean, draw on the trope of the coconut, such that a close encounter with Shakespeare is still reliant on a particular display of English literariness understood to exist in a binary relation to a putative Africanness. This despite our own literary archive, steeped in activism, which suggests that Shakespeare has been far more profound for the South Africans who have closely encountered 'him'. More than this, I want to follow through on the old coconut logic: is there by now a kind of artificiality, an inauthenticity, a hollowness at the core of such a display, which is activated because of the ongoing valency of a pernicious but, in real terms, ongoing binary? This discussion ultimately asks what the place of Shakespeare is, in post-apartheid South African public culture.

I suggest that precisely the kind of problematic binary thinking which animates the original idea of the coconut might now infuse the public representation of the experience of Shakespeare's texts. Although this binary logic is theoretically suspect and an inaccurate model for how identification occurs at the level of the everyday, it is being reinscribed in post-apartheid South Africa because it does in fact accurately reflect an experience of the world; it speaks of the ongoing hierarchies of social and economic power. And Shakespeare belongs firmly to the privileged half of the binary, despite 'his' regional history as a literary, political, and, indeed, personal resource for discourses of resistance. Daily post-apartheid experience is trumping literary colonial history.

A more concrete way of posing this coconut question is to ask, can Shakespeare, who has reached Africans through a particular historical process, ever be free of 'his' colonial masters despite the existence of a rich African Shakespearean tradition, in the context of current relations of social and economic power in the country and in the world? If, as the range of South African texts discussed below suggest, the answer may be no, then a third definition of 'coconut' might be useful for us in South Africa. If the first meaning we have is of the person black on the outside but white on the inside, and the second is the idea I have been propounding, that coconuts should be seen as Africans throughout our history who have lived an imbricated, implicated identity, then the third meaning might be encapsulated by the idea of someone anxiously trying to be something he is not, and in the related reasons why someone would try to alter herself. These reasons return us to the material conditions of the present, which are at once the inheritance of our history and the consequences of our current choices. Of course, the latter cannot easily be lifted out of the former.

Coconut (2007)

As we saw in chapter one, Kopano Matlwa's debut novel, *Coconut*,[1] details the hopes and aspirations, and the costs, of two young women's searches for identity in South Africa in 2007. One, Ofilwe, belongs to the generation whose parents have acquired upper-middle-class status, and the other, Fikile, aspires to this status. The novel makes it clear that both young women have internalised aspects of whiteness, in different ways, and to different effects. They are, in their own ways, coconuts. Ofilwe feels alienated from her parents' culture and language, and Fikile loathes where she finds herself located culturally. Fikile's Shakespeare-quoting uncle is another kind of coconut. Uncle constantly quotes or paraphrases Shakespeare as the ultimate expression of his distress:

> *'Oh, I am fortune's fool!' Uncle would begin, whimpering.*

> *'Yes, Uncle,' I would sigh. No, Uncle, I would think. Not again, not now, please. I had homework to do …*

> *'I have lost all my mirth, the earth seems sterile.'*

> *'Yes, Uncle,' I would say again, for that was all that was expected from me … during these laments when Uncle would spew out pieces of Shakespeare as if he thought them up himself while lost in the abyss of his sorry existence …*[2]

> *'I am dying, Fikile, dying … When beggars die, there are no comets seen,' he would sob …*

'Yes, Uncle.'

'I am a godly man, Fikile.'

'Yes, Uncle.'

'I am an honest man, Fikile.'

'Yes, Uncle.'

'A righteous man, Fikile.'

'Yes, Uncle.'

'That it should come to this!'

'Yes, Uncle.'

'I struggle each day to keep a free and open nature.'

'Yes, Uncle.'

'The world is grown so bad that wrens make prey where eagles dare not perch.'

At this point, of course, I had long stopped listening ... He was speaking to himself ...[3]

The reasons for Uncle's distress are implicated in their Shakespearean expression. Uncle's knowledge of Shakespeare is a signifier of his proficiency in English, and thus a trace marker or remnant of the privileged education he had access to as a child, when he was taken into the household of the white family that employed his mother as a domestic worker. Very specifically, though, for Fikile, herself unashamedly aspirant to 'white' economic and social privilege, Uncle's Shakespeare is an empty signifier. It comprises an arguably poignant but ultimately empty display of Englishness and 'white' erudition. His ongoing monologue of quotes serves as a marker of his failure to achieve the promise of advancement implicit in the acquisition of a certain kind of education.

Uncle's distress is about his work situation, where he is being cynically used as 'window dressing' in the post-apartheid government's Black Economic Empowerment policy. It is Shakespeare who enabled this situation, marking Uncle as a black man with specific, although practically useless, talents:

> 'They use me, Fikile ... I sit in my chair at the security desk and read my books ... I love my books ... My Hamlet, my kings – Richard and Lear – my Julius Caesar, my Antony and Cleopatra, my beautiful but yet so tragic Romeo and Juliet ... Ah, but some rise by sin and some by virtue fall ...
>
> Oh Fikile, when Mr Dix approached me at my humble security desk and inquired about the books I read, I was only honoured to share with him the might, the mastery and supremacy that lay within those pages ...
>
> But he is mad that trusts in the tameness of a wolf, a horse's health, a boy's love or a whore's oath. I was a fool ... I should have known those heavy white

> men in their dry-cleaned suits were not interested in
> my sonnets but in my black skin.' [4]

Uncle's English, and specifically 'his' Shakespeare, indicate his ability to perform a proficiency that does not in fact result in anything. Mr Dix occasionally lends him a suit and takes him along to business meetings where he is introduced as a senior member of the business, forbidden from participating in the discussion, and whisked out of the room under the pretense of an urgent call as soon as possible. Uncle will never be a successful businessman, even as his English, exemplified by 'his' Shakespeare, enables him to pretend that he is. It is his Shakespeare's performance value, together with Uncle's desperation – that is, the fact precisely that he is not what he seems, that he is poor – that makes him useful to his bosses (Fikile is narrating here):

> *'I am a man more sinned against than sinning.' Sniff-sniff. Bullshit. Absolute bullshit! Uncle knew very well that from that first day when Mr Dix asked him to read him passages from his books and asked him to recite the poetry, Uncle lauded over everyone; he was being interviewed, assessed and evaluated for the position of black fake senior partner/CEO/co-founder/financial director or whatever position it was that spoke of transformation at Lentso Communications ...*

> *Uncle was just another hungry black man, hungry for a piece of the pie like the rest of us ... Uncle is a liar and a fake ... He's pathetic as a security guard and probably would have been fired by now if they hadn't found out that he spoke English so well.* [5]

Uncle's English is a marker of education and the necessary element for attainment of what Fikile calls *'the soft life'*, which *'everyone ... yearned for'*, [6] even as his propensity for displaying this education by quoting Shakespeare emphasises his lack of attainment of financial success. Uncle is the failed version of the earlier, mission-schooled, upwardly mobile young man who, through the promise of Western education, would further the 'progress' of himself and, as a leader, his people, towards modernity. This figure, an important one in the history of writing in English in the region, as well as in the development of a political leadership and a colonial petit bourgeoisie, is specifically gendered, a point made by Fikile when she mentions that his sister, as talented as he, was not thought worthy of education by the white family.

Fikile has no respect for what Uncle's Shakespeare signifies. Like one of Johnson's versions of Plaatje, Fikile depicts her uncle as a *'Yes-Man'*. [7] For her, his empty displays confirm that he is *'[s]uch a twerp ... Such a sorry, pathetic, little twerp ... I loathed this man'*. [8] The reason she hates him so much is that when he is particularly inconsolable – when he is most steeped in his lachrymose Shakespeare and has *'that sorry look'* when he comes home from work – he sexually abuses her, which she experiences as 'comforting' him: [9] *'I hated that Uncle was such a sorry and pathetic and weak man and hated even more that I was the only one who was able to comfort him.'* [10] His sexual abuse of Fikile is a sign of his loss of manhood, and his love of Shakespeare facilitates the expression of his failure and emasculation.

Uncle is a poor *'investment'* [11] for the white family who educated him, and for his community, an economic signifier that has everything to do with what English means for Fikile. It is crucial to note, however, that Fikile is not rejecting the aspiration to whiteness she sees him as having squandered.

> Uncle could have had it all and he screwed it up. The
> Kinsleys did so much for Uncle even though they didn't
> have to. I mean, he was only their domestic worker's son
> and yet they treated him like he was one of their own ...
> If only they had known that all the money they were
> investing in tuition, school uniforms, piano lessons and
> expensive encyclopaedias would one day go to waste.
> If only they had invested that money in me instead of
> Uncle ... I knew that if I had been given half the chance
> Uncle had been given I would never have turned out to
> be a disappointment ... I knew that if I was given the
> chance to meet the Kinsleys, then all my problems would
> be solved, for they would surely ask me to move into
> their home right then and there and change my name to
> something cute like Sarah Kinsley. [12]

As she dresses herself for work in the morning, putting in her
green contact lenses and applying her skin-lightening cream,
Fikile observes:

> [P]erhaps it is for the better that the conditions in this
> dump never improve. They can serve as a constant
> reminder to me of what I do not want to be: black,
> dirty and poor. This bucket [where she washes] can
> be a daily motivator for me to keep working towards
> where I will someday be: white, rich and happy. [13]

She is grooming herself towards this end, and, crucially, this
involves educating herself in English.

> I am now more confident in everything I do and am no
> longer uncertain of my capabilities. Nothing intimidates

me. I have even started speaking in the English language even when I do not need to. I am no longer concerned with what I sound like because I have come to believe that I sound like any other English-speaking person. I use words like 'facetious' and 'filial' in everyday speech and speak English boldly ... Not like Uncle, who spews out fragments of Shakespeare that make little sense to him or anyone else, but with insight and understanding. [14]

It is not Uncle's aspiration that disgusts Fikile. It is his failed aspiration, and Shakespeare is the signifier of this failure. Shakespeare is the display of a veneer of Englishness; by virtue of its incomprehensibility, it is in fact evidence of what it is trying to conceal, a hollowness and lack of substance. This is in opposition to Fikile's 'insight[ful]' use of English. Her comment, that she now feels confident of sounding *'like any other English-speaking person'*, speaks to a long social history of accent in South Africa, and to the types of English spoken by most South Africans, now recognised as its own regional variant with the publication of the Oxford University Press *Dictionary of South African English* in 2002. This legitimation is lost on Fikile, though, who is striving to differentiate herself from most South Africans and enter a caste whose markers of belonging include various aspects of what Fikile identifies as whiteness: money, designer labels, Western culture (symbolised by Avril Lavigne on the cover of her latest *Girlfriend* magazine), happiness, cleanliness, dignity, and, of course, English spoken in a specific way, all the time (not just as a lingua franca or when talking to monolingual white South Africans). Fikile knows that *'the accent matters'*, [15] as do real-life young South Africans. [16] Fikile's private fantasy of selfhood, her self-fashioning, embodies the centrality of Englishness to her aspirations:

> My name is Fiks Twala. I have a second name, Fikile,
> which I never use because many find it too difficult to
> pronounce ... I grew up in white environments for the
> most part of my life, from primary school right up to
> high school. Many people think I am foreign, from the
> UK or somewhere there. I think it is because my accent is
> so perfect and my manner so refined. Yes, I have always
> been different. I never could relate to other black South
> Africans ... It's never been an issue for me though. I
> guess you do not miss something you have never known
> ...
>
> I lived in England for a while, Mummy and Daddy still
> lecture there. I couldn't stand the weather, absolutely
> dreadful, so I moved back here ... It's harder here though,
> you have to do everything for yourself. You can't trust
> anybody, not with all the crime and corruption. But ja,
> it's home, what can I say? [17]

Her motto is 'Fake it 'til you make it'. [18]

The kitchen staff at the restaurant where she works, all of
whom would be working-class black people like Fikile herself,
respond to her by shaking their heads and saying, 'Shame'. She
responds, 'Stupid people ... why are they feeling sorry for me?' [19]

Even as Fikile cannot see what she is betraying, Matlwa is clear
that 'authentic' working-class Africanness is poor compensation
for hundreds of years of oppression and concomitant deprivation,
even as she is aware of the complexities of the identity and class
positions that have resulted. Fikile's co-worker, Ayanda, is a
child of the post-apartheid privilege meted out to the small black
middle class. He is working at the restaurant to try to reconnect
with the authenticity he feels his privileged upbringing has cost

him. Ayanda has a run-in with a racist white patron who wants a cheese sandwich without the cheese. Their interaction results in Ayanda's outburst, which Fikile calls *'talking all sorts of revolution shit'*: [20]

> *'They feel nothing. They see nothing, absolutely nothing wrong with the great paradox in this country. Ten per cent of them still living on ninety per cent of the land, ninety per cent of us still living on ten per cent of the land ... Any fool ... can see that there is a gross contradiction in this country.'* What was Ayanda talking about? He lived in some loft his parents had bought him in Morningside [a previously whites-only upper-middle-class suburb] ...

> *'How many of them do you hear saying that they want to leave the country? ... "Oh the crime! Oh the poverty!" ... So why don't they leave? Why the hell did they come here in the first place? ... If they want to leave, I say the sooner the better.'*

> I knew he didn't mean that. He didn't mean any of it. Ayanda had tons of white friends ... Ayanda had gone to a white school, lived in white neighbourhoods all his life. He had the life that everybody dreamed of. The ass was just talking out of his arse. And we all knew it. I did, the kitchen staff did, and he did. So after that, he got back to work. [21]

The acquisition of the social and economic capital experienced by Fikile as whiteness has real, life-altering power. While English is crucial to this process, and Fikile works hard to fake her English identity until she can properly acquire it, Shakespeare bears a different relation to it. While Shakespeare stands for proficiency in English, 'he' signifies, specifically, useless knowledge and a particular kind of display. Unlike English, Shakespeare is flashy but ultimately empty of real content and so empty of real power.

Has Shakespeare's display value become the defining element of 'his' post-apartheid South African incarnation? Has 'he' become the marker, not just of the old meaning of the coconut, but, in the context of democratic and neo-liberal South Africa, the failed coconut? *Coconut*'s analysis of 'white' privilege, accessible by those black men and women who can perform the relevant, meaningful markers of Englishness, is pertinent and incisive. Shakespeare, as the exemplar of English, stands for access to this privilege. But Uncle's mobilisation of the quotes to express his 'sorry state', the state in which he abuses a child, stands also for his failed attempt, his partial and ultimately unsuccessful access. Fikile does not reject the aspirations encoded in Uncle's Shakespeare. Indeed, she is passionately committed to achieving them. What she does not buy is that Shakespeare is a viable pathway to this social mobility and, more vitally, a relevant marker of the psychic authenticity she feels precedes her right to this mobility.

A coconut at Polokwane

Fikile is a canny young woman who has understood how privilege operates in post-apartheid South Africa and is single-minded in her desire to better her social standing. By embracing 'white' Englishness, she has ensured that she will always be aspiring to something she can never quite be, a version of Ngugi wa Thiong'o's colonised African mind. [22] Crucially, Matlwa's novel explored these issues when South Africa was under the leadership of a president who is famous for quoting Shakespeare most specifically, as well as other canonised English writers, in his political speeches. In South African public discourse that dominated at the time *Coconut* was published, and which reached a kind of a climax after he lost his position at Polokwane, Thabo Mbeki's Shakespeare appears as a signifier of his self-fashioning and concomitant alienation from his constituency, standing for his positioning in an either/or formulation where a leader is either in a personal relationship with Shakespeare and all 'he' represents, or in touch with 'the' African people. Sometimes Shakespeare is mentioned along with other canonical writers, but Shakespeare is always present in this discussion. Like Uncle's Shakespeare, Mbeki's Shakespeare becomes emblematic of a fatal character flaw, in a new twist on the heroic identification with a Shakespearean tragic hero we have seen so far.

Writing at the time of the ANC presidential succession saga, in December 2007, author Rian Malan assessed Mbeki's career. Commenting on his image in South Africa as being more concerned with his global commitments than with what was happening in the country he was supposed to be leading, Malan writes tellingly of the display value of Mbeki's literate speeches:

> At times, he seemed to be living a fantasy in which he starred as a great statesman, descending from the sky in the presidential jet and marching down a red carpet into a forest of microphones to deliver a speech laced with quotes from Yeats and Shakespeare, leaving the western world shaken to its racist core by the sight of an African more suave and civilised than it could ever hope to be. [23]

Relevant to Matlwa's depiction of an unimpressed Fikile, he adds, 'I say western advisedly, because it remains unclear whether Africans are impressed by this sort of intellectual flash. The audience whose approval Mbeki most deeply craved was white and western.' [24] Indeed, political journalist Xolela Mangcu, who places himself in the same intellectual tradition as Mbeki, comments, '[W]e have a president who at every opportunity is always more interested in how clever he is than in empathizing with the rest of the population.' [25] Mbeki lost the party's presidential position to Jacob Zuma, who has been cast as a populist, and whose victory was a clear indication from the ANC membership that they were fed up with Mbeki's management style. Commenting on Zuma's first policy speech as ANC president, journalist Fiona Forde described Zuma's style and content:

> Zuma ... made his way to the podium with unmistakable authority ... [H]e spoke with clarity and in a deliberate tone. His choice of words was simple, yet meaningful. There was not a word of Shakespeare this year ... Instead, he delivered a straightforward statement and used his voice and not verbosity to give emphasis at every punchline. [26]

By inference, Mbeki's Shakespeare is obscure, elitist, and obfuscating. It symbolises the reason why he lost popular support and organisational power. The charge of elitism, so encapsulated in Mbeki's penchant for Shakespeare, implicitly links him to 'the West' and all its putative interests – big business, 'white' culture – in a binary formulation where Zuma's plain speaking marks him as a man of 'the people'. [27] Reporting on the 2007 ANC national conference held at the University of Limpopo in Polokwane, at which Mbeki lost the presidency to Zuma, Kevin

Bloom and Phillip de Wet took a moment to reminisce about Mbeki's image. They emphasise his English (both his education and acculturation, and his use of language), which sums up his contrast to Zuma and, and in, his class interests:

> 'But he's so well spoken!' That was a favourite phrase at the dinner tables of white South Africa, circa midsummer 1997 ... Only ten short years ago, many of those who today equate Zuma with the impending apocalypse were heaping praise on the sophisticate who would inherit the country from Nelson Mandela. Mbeki, it was widely quoted, held a master's degree in economics from a British university [Sussex], the suits he wore were from Savile Row, there were even photographs of him in his younger days smoking a good English pipe. Such sentiments were further entrenched when, after Mbeki took power, he liberally salted his official speeches with references to Pliny the Elder, William Shakespeare and William Butler Yeats. Here was a man ... with whom foreign investors and Caucasians everywhere could identify. [28, 29]

Similarly, in Allister Sparks's assessment, Zuma

> is essentially a man of the people, with a charm and warmth that endears him to the crowds. He would not be the philosopher president. You would not hear him quoting Yeats or Shakespeare or delivering speeches of literary grandeur, but he has his ear to the ground and he knows what's going on. As the Afrikaners used to say of their political equivalents,

> *Hy weet waar die volk se hart klop* [he knows where the
> people's heart beats]. He is clever, but not too clever
> ... [30]

Read together with Matlwa's devastating assessment of African
men who quote Shakespeare, Mbeki appears to be in danger of
being called a failed coconut himself. However, as Isabel Hofmeyr
has pointed out, the use of Shakespeare in political speeches by
the post-apartheid political leadership continues a genre that was
developed in the colonial mission schools. [31] The display value
of the Shakespeare text in such a context is more than window
dressing; it enters into a rhetorical tradition that makes use of
the social power accrued to Englishness, for its own ends. This
tradition, as Hofmeyr notes, is under-appreciated. Instead,
Mbeki's Shakespeare is touted in the public realm as an indicator
of his sense of himself as educated and erudite, as anglicised,
implicitly a sign of his failure to connect with his constituency.

Journalistic impatience with Mbeki's Shakespeare, which
peaked during post-Polokwane reports, was in evidence before
the 2007 conference, again as shorthand for all that was wrong
with Mbeki's leadership. Political correspondent Vukani Mde
began his 2006 assessment of Mbeki's State of the Nation address
of that year by rejecting first the poet and then the president who
needs him:

> I've never liked Shakespeare. He is of very limited
> use to the modern writer. He wrote too much on
> too many subjects, and on many occasions made
> himself guilty of the twin infractions for which no
> writer can be forgiven: repetition and contradiction.
> In fact his oeuvre suffers from the same literary
> and philosophical pitfalls that litter the Bible.

They are both impossible to quote without fear of contradiction, or worse, ridicule. But while I've always tolerated the Bible as a joint effort between people with different agendas, I make no such allowances for a lone Englishman from Stratford-upon-Avon who should have known better. I just don't do Shakespeare. You can imagine my dismay then, when I realised President Thabo Mbeki meant to base his state of the nation literary effort on these two unreliable sources. I've just never understood our president's devotion to the man's writing. He runs to him at the slightest provocation, in increasingly silly attempts to lend poetic gravitas to the prosaic work of government. But poetry as a mode of communicating the ordinary unfortunately delivers ever-diminishing returns ... I just fell asleep in the end ... It was torture most foul. [32]

In an ironic repeat of a familiar colonial conflation which saw Shakespeare's texts as the secular equivalent of the Bible, and equally important for the civilisation of the natives, [33] Mde here addresses Shakespeare and the Bible as twin sources of an irrelevant, imposed, overrated culture. The symbolic power of this culture, disavowed as it may be by Mde, nevertheless resonates through this critique in his inability to resist the temptation to use Shakespeare himself. It is not just Shakespeare's pithy epithetic quality, as in the final sentence quoted above, that is available to this journalist writing in English. He concludes his article by turning Shakespeare against Mbeki, and benefits from both the poetry and the emblematic truth-value of the texts:

> When historians chronicle [Mbeki's] so-called Age
> of Hope, they may praise faintly for the stunning
> successes, but will damn him for the devastating
> failures. Shakespeare said: 'The evil that men do lives
> after them, but the good is oft interred with their
> bodies.' So it shall be with Mbeki. Macbeth's lament
> [quoted by Mbeki in his speech] ends thus: 'Life is
> but a walking shadow. A poor player, that struts and
> frets his hour upon the stage and then is heard no
> more. 'Tis a tale told by an idiot, full of sound and
> fury, signifying nothing.' Like a mid-term state of the
> nation speech. [34]

Mde deploys the very authority he deplores, in order to perform
the same rhetorical flourishes for which he damns Mbeki.
Shakespeare clearly still has both symbolic and poetic clout.
Mde is relying upon this clout to invest his statement 'I just don't
do Shakespeare' with provocation. At the same time, he does
'do' Shakespeare, in order to undo Mbeki's presentation and,
implicitly, Mbeki's self-presentation. The attack is as personal as
it is political.

It is instructive that another text in the public realm at the
time of the succession battle for presidency of the ANC when
Mbeki's reign was being assessed, this time a political cartoon, [35]
also invokes his well-known Shakespearean proclivities in order
to turn them against him in a critique that aims at more than his
political presence:

The reference in the second frame of the bottom line to Zuma's 'comeback' 'explains' his ability to survive rape and corruption charges to become president of the ANC. Eve's reprimand 'Didn't we tell you to stay away from beetroot?' references the then-Health Minister Manto Tshabalala-Msimang's ('Lady Manto') notorious comments about how to treat HIV, in the context of Mbeki's ongoing tacit support for AIDS denialism. Mbeki first accessed denialist positions on the Internet.

Mbeki's Shakespearean quote 'I conjure you ... ' is met with Mother Anderson's 'Tell him to speak English'. Thus the cartoonists comment, not only on Shakespeare's incomprehensibility, but on Mbeki's leadership style, from his highfalutin speeches to his sometimes incomprehensible take on key issues such as HIV, or Zimbabwe. In order to fully appreciate the humour, a reader has to be familiar with Mbeki's reputation as depicted by Malan. Crucially, the reader does not have to be familiar with *Macbeth*, only with the most famous elements of the play in common circulation. *Macbeth* is the play most likely to be recognised by post-apartheid South Africans, since it has been the most popular setwork, not least because it is short and, according to teachers who have to present it to schoolchildren, full of action (not wordiness). [36]

This cartoon generates some of its humour by playing on Mbeki's characteristic love of Shakespeare, and using *Macbeth* to comment on a struggle for power that dominated the nation's public discourse for weeks, cleverly linking the play's concerns with legitimate leadership, political and personal betrayal, and murderous political machinations to similar issues in the ANC presidential succession saga (sans the literal murder, but very much in keeping with the tone of the events). But it also generates humour at a much more private cost to Mbeki, a man whose public persona is steeped in his performance of familiarity with the civilisation Shakespeare represents, as we have seen. One of the cartoon's subtexts is the president's murderous stance on HIV; it ends, after all, with Mother Anderson's nightmare culminating in a vision of the health minister responsible for implementing Mbeki's denialism and perpetuating a refusal to embrace Western science. Mbeki is accused of practising precisely the kind of superstitious, 'heathen' behaviour commonly associated with stereotypes of the tribal African. It is instructive, then, to note that of all Shakespeare's plays, *Macbeth* is the one now most commonly proclaimed to have 'relevance' to Africans because of its tribal Scottish context and because, precisely, of the witches [37] (in colonial times the play most 'relevant' to the African elite, as Can Themba suggests, was *Julius Caesar*). The *Madam & Eve* cartoon thus at once draws on Mbeki's erudition, and disciplines him for it, in the face of his behaviour regarding HIV, in which he assumes an anti-Western binary positioning when it suits his emotional and/or policy needs, even as his deployment of Shakespeare acknowledges a respect for Western cultural norms.

What this analysis demonstrates once again is the prevalence of old binaries that by now should have no place in the new South Africa, one of which is Europe/Africa, which corresponds to associations with science/traditional medicine. Mbeki's quoting of Shakespeare is revealed to be a veneer, beneath which his 'true' African self is revealed in his irresponsible, anti-democratic behaviour, his high-handed, ignorant, and deadly approach to the HIV crisis.

Thus, despite actual literatures which provide content to a truly Africanised Shakespeare, and which bespeak a syncretic South African identification process that is a more accurate reflection of how we are made than our history's various attempts to cordon off cultures from one another, [38] the associations with public deployments of knowledge of the Shakespeare text suggest that Shakespeare does not have substantially more than display value in the current South African public arena. What is on display when Shakespeare is displayed is an affiliation with a positioning of privilege and concomitant socio-economic power, but no meaningful content, if not actively negative content. Thus Shakespeare is by now first and foremost the indicator of where cultural and economic power lie, which, because of ongoing relations of power that have not altered with the advent of democracy, tend to be constructed in a binary relation to a putative Africanness. Because of 'his' public image, Shakespeare easily becomes the ultimate tinsel in the window dressing, a more important literary, political, and psychological history in the region notwithstanding. Is there room for a close encounter with Shakespeare in post-apartheid South Africa which can be represented in any but the most personal terms? Has Shakespeare grown, not just old, but white, here? After all this time, and after all this personal, political, and literary history, is 'he' the fluff on the coconut?

Endnotes

INTRODUCTION

1 From I. de Kok, *Seasonal Fires: new and selected poems* (New York: Seven Stories Press, 2006), p. 94–95.

2 Minelle Mahtani, 'Mixed Metaphors: Positioning "Mixed Race" Identity', in *Situating 'Race' and Racisms in Space, Time, and Theory: Critical Essays for Activists and Scholars*, eds Jo-Anne Lee & John Lutz (Montreal: McGill-Queens University Press, 2005), pp. 77–93; p. 90 n. 1.

3 'Apples' is a term used by Native Americans, and 'bananas' by Chinese about Chinese Singaporeans – see Tracy L. Mack, 'What Can You Learn from a Rainbow?', *Interracial Voice*, March/April 1999. Accessed December 2008, http://www.webcom.com/~intvoice/tracy.html.

4 'Rotten coconut' denotes someone who is brown on the outside and black on the inside, as in Indians who perform a hip-hop identity – see Nitasha Sharma, 'Rotten Coconuts and Other Strange Fruits', *Samar* 14 (Fall/Winter 2001). Accessed January 2008, http://www.samarmagazine.org/archive/article.php?id=62. Sharma comments that while the fruit metaphors for acting white 'are perfectly healthy ... this reference stigmatized those seen as "trying to be black" as "rotten" and "downwardly" assimilating'.

5 Sarfraz Manzoor, 'The Coconut Conundrum', *The Guardian* 30 July 2007. Accessed December 2008, http://www.sarfrazmanzoor.co.uk.

6 Catherine McKinney, '"If I Speak English Does it Make Me Less Black Anyway?" "Race" and English in South African Desegregated Schools', *English Academy Review* 24.2 (2007): 6–24.

7 Such as David Attwell's *Rewriting Modernity: Studies in Black South African Literary History* (Pietermaritzburg: UKZN Press, 2005) and Isabel Hofmeyr's *The Portable Bunyan: A Transnational History of 'The Pilgrim's Progress'* (Princeton: Princeton University Press, 2004).

8 A. Mngxitama, 'Coconut Kids Have Lost Touch with Their Roots', *City Press* 30 September 2007, p. 26.

9 L. de Kock, 'South Africa in the Global Imaginary: An Introduction', in *South Africa in the Global Imaginary*, eds L. de Kock, L. Bethlehem & S. Laden (Pretoria: Unisa Press, 2004), pp. 1–31, especially pp. 21.

10 For an example of how Shakespeare and performances of Africanness have worked together, see N. Distiller, '"We're black, stupid": uMabatha and the New South Africa on the World Stage', in *Under Construction: 'Race' and Identity in South Africa Today*, eds N. Distiller & M. Steyn (Cape Town: Heinemann, 2004), pp. 149–162.

CHAPTER 1 Shakespeare in English, English in South Africa

1 K. Matlwa, *Coconut* (Johannesburg: Jacana Media, 2007), p. 31. Italics in the original.

2 Matlwa, *Coconut*, pp. 135–136. Italics in the original.

3 Matlwa, *Coconut*, pp. 40–41. Italics in the original.

4 Matlwa, *Coconut*, p. 54. Italics in the original.

5 Matlwa, *Coconut*, p. 55.

6 For more on the role of gender in the early history of English education in South Africa, see N. Distiller, *South Africa, Shakespeare, and Post-colonial Culture* (Lampeter: Edwin Mellen, 2005), chapters 1 and 3. For a direct comment on the importance of linguistic activism, not mediated through fiction, see K. Matlwa, 'Call me a Coconut but African Tongues are Destined for Obscurity', *Sunday Times* 7 October 2007, p. 29. Here Matlwa comes much closer to personally owning the book's distress at the positioning of Africanness as inferior to Englishness and its whiteness: 'I can say this with confidence because I know.'

7   Matlwa, *Coconut*, p. 176. Italics in the original.

8   See S. Nuttall & C.-A. Michael, 'Imagining the Present', in
    Senses of Culture: South African Culture Studies, eds S. Nuttall &
    C.-A. Michael (Oxford: Oxford University Press, 2000), pp. 1–27, for
    the first sustained attempt to theorise a post-apartheid re-visioning
    of cultural identities and histories in South Africa.

9   *New Zimbabwe News*, 'Malema v BBC Journalist', 8 April 2010.
    See this site for a video of the incident as well as a transcript.
    Accessed May 2011, http://www.newzimbabwe.com/news/news.
    aspx?newsID=2201.

10 This is discussed in chapter five.

11 As examples of his invocations of racialised colonial rhetoric:
    Malema said to the South African Students' Congress in 2009, 'The
    rich keep getting richer and it is white males who continue to own
    the means of production in the country. Not even Tokyo [Sexwale],
    who is the minister of human settlements [and a highly successful
    businessman], is an owner. Tokyo is owing the white *baas* [boss]
    because he wants to borrow from the banks. Who owns the banks?
    Tokyo is a rich man, but he doesn't own.' ('How Malema Made
    His Millions,' *Sunday Times* 21 February 2010. Accessed May 2011,
    http://www.timeslive.co.za/sundaytimes/article318330.ece/How-
    Malema-made-his-millions.) Malema also sounded particularly
    Mugabe-esque on an election platform on 7 May 2011. Speaking
    about white people, he said: '"We must take the land without
    paying. They took our land without paying. Once we agree they
    stole our land, we can agree they are criminals and must be treated
    as such," he said to cheers from a crowd of about 3 000 people at
    the Galeshewe stadium, just outside Kimberley.' ('Malema: White
    People are Criminals', *IOL News* 8 May 2011. Accessed May 2011,
    http://www.iol.co.za/news/white-people-are-criminals-
    malema-1.1066339.) He repeatedly presents himself as speaking
    for the poor and disenfranchised. At the same time he has been
    embroiled in controversies for the luxury homes, cars, and goods
    that he owns ('Malema's Millions', *The Star*, 19 Feb 2010. Accessed
    May 2011, http://www.iol.co.za/news/politics/pics-malema-s-
    millions-1.473967) and for the corrupt business and tender practices
    with which he has been associated ('How Malema Made His
    Millions').

12 For example, the way Zuma deployed his Zulu identity to defend himself against rape charges (see T. Waetjen & G. Mare, 'Tradition's Desire: The Politics of Culture in the Rape Trial of Jacob Zuma', *Concerned Africa Scholars Bulletin* 84 [2010]: 52–61).

13 For an extended investigation into the history of Shakespeare in writing in South Africa, from Plaatje forward, see Distiller, *South Africa, Shakespeare, and Post-colonial Culture*.

14 N. Rhodes, *Shakespeare and the Origins of English* (Oxford: Oxford University Press, 2004); M. Arnold, *Culture and Anarchy*, ed. S. Lipman (New Haven & London: Yale University Press, 1994 [1869]); G. Viswanathan, *Masks of Conquest: Literary Study and British Rule in India* (New York: Columbia University Press, 1989); T. Eagleton, *Literary Theory: An Introduction*, 2nd edition (Oxford: Blackwell, 1996 [1983]).

15 P. Widdowson, ed., *Re-reading English* (London & New York: Methuen, 1982); Viswanathan, *Masks of Conquest*; Eagleton, *Literary Theory*, pp. 15–46; Rhodes, *Shakespeare and the Origins*, p. 192.

16 C. Belsey, *The Subject of Tragedy: Identity and Difference in Renaissance Drama* (London & New York: Methuen, 1985); J. Dollimore & A. Sinfield (eds), *Political Shakespeare: New Essays in Cultural Materialism* (Manchester & New York: Manchester University Press, 1985); M. Orkin, *Shakespeare Against Apartheid* (Craighall: Ad. Donker, 1987); J. Dollimore, *Radical Tragedy*, 2nd edition (Hertfordshire: Harvester Wheatsheaf, 1989).

17 G. Taylor, *Reinventing Shakespeare: A Cultural History from the Restoration to the Present* (Oxford: Oxford University Press, 1989); M. Evans, *Signifying Nothing: Truth's True Contexts in Shakespeare's Texts*, 2nd edition (Hertfordshire: Harvester Wheatsheaf, 1989); M. Bristol, *Shakespeare's America, America's Shakespeare* (London & New York: Routledge, 1990); T. Hawkes, *Meaning by Shakespeare* (London & New York: Routledge, 1992).

18 For two informed, intelligent examples, see J. Bate, *The Genius of Shakespeare* (London & Basingstoke: Picador, 1997); and C. Belsey, *Why Shakespeare?* (Hampshire & New York: Palgrave Macmillan, 2007). M. Garber, *Shakespeare After All* (New York: Anchor Books, 2004), offers perhaps one of the most measured accounts of the imbrications of Shakespeare with modern Anglo-American culture, along with the recognition of the historical, that is, material and

political, trajectory of the development of 'his' current, apparently transcendent and immutable, meanings.

19 See 'South Africa Reinstates Authors', *BBC News* 22 April 2001. Accessed August 2005, http://news.bbc.co.uk/hi/english/ entertainment/arts/newsid_1291000/1291396.stm. See also 'Keeping SA Schools Safe from Literature', *Sunday Times* n.d. Accessed August 2005, http://www.suntimes.co.za/education/ setworks/index.asp.

20 Anthony Sampson, editor of *Drum* magazine when it hosted and developed some of the most productive Englished and Shakespearised South African writers in the 1950s (see Distiller, *South Africa, Shakespeare, and Post-colonial Culture*), responded to the suggestion that Shakespeare be removed from school syllabi by pointing to Shakespeare's presence on Robben Island as an anti-apartheid force. ('O, What Men Dare Do', *The Observer* 22 April 2001. Accessed June 2001, http://www.observer.co.uk/comment/ story/0,6903,476514,00.html.) For more on 'the Robben Island Shakespeare', also known as 'the Robben Island Bible', see D. Schalkwyk, 'Hamlet's Dreams', *Social Dynamics* 32.2 (2006): 1–21.

21 For perhaps the most famous examples, see Ngugi wa Thiong'o, *Decolonising the Mind: The Politics of Language in African Literature* (London: James Currey, 1986) and *Moving the Centre: The Struggle for Cultural Freedoms* (London: James Currey, 1993).

22 'Du Plessis reports that isiZulu at 23 per cent has the highest numbers of speakers, with isiXhosa following at 18 per cent and Afrikaans at 14 per cent. English only comes in at number five with 9 per cent. According to the 1991 census (although these data have been questioned, says du Plessis), roughly 42 per cent of the South African population claim to speak/understand/read/write English with the same percentage claiming to speak/understand/read/ write Afrikaans (p. 101).' (M. Green, 'Translating the Nation: From Plaatje to Mpe', *Journal of Southern African Studies* 34.2 [June 2008]: 325–342, p. 325 fn. 1, quoting T. du Plessis, 'South Africa: From Two to Eleven Official Languages', in *Multilingualism and Government: Belgium, Luxembourg, Switzerland, Former Yugoslavia, South Africa*, eds K. Deprez & T. du Plessis [Pretoria: Van Schaik, 2000], pp. 95–110.)

23 K. Sole, 'Class, Continuity and Change in Black South African Literature, 1948–1960', in *Labour, Townships and Protest: Studies in the Social History of the Witwatersrand*, ed. B. Bozzoli (Johannesburg: Ravan Press, 2001), pp. 143–182; A. Oboe, 'Of Books and The Book: The Evangelical Mission in South African Literature', in *Colonies – Missions – Cultures – in the English-speaking World*, ed. G. Stilz (Tubingen: Stauffenburg Verlag, 2001), pp. 235–246; M. Chapman, *Southern African Literatures* (London & New York: Longman, 1996); B.V. Jordan, 'Using the English Language, South African Writers Fight Back against the Colonizers' Writings and Philosophies' (PhD diss., Albany State University, 1995); E. Mphahlele, 'An Apple for the Teachers', *Tribute* (August 1994): 117–118; M.V. Mzamane, 'Culture and Social Environment in the Pre-colonial Era', *Tydskrif vir Letterkunde* 46.1 (2009): 192–205; P.V. Shava, *A People's Voice: Black South African Writing in the Twentieth Century* (London and Athens, OH: Zed & Ohio State University Press, 1989); A.C. Jordan, *Towards an African Literature: The Emergence of Literary Form in Xhosa* (Berkeley, Los Angeles, & London: University of California Press, 1973).

24 L. de Kock, 'Sitting for the Civilization Test: The Making(s) of a Civil Imaginary in Colonial South Africa', *Poetics Today* 22.2 (2001): 391–412, p. 398; L. de Kock, *Civilising Barbarians: Missionary Narrative and African Textual Response in Nineteenth-Century South Africa* (Johannesburg: Wits University Press, 1996); G.A. Duncan, *Lovedale: Coercive Agency* (Pietermaritzburg: Cluster, 2003).

25 De Kock, *Civilising Barbarians*, p. 30.

26 E. Mphahlele, 'Prometheus in Chains: The Fate of English in South Africa', *English Academy Review* 2.1 (1984): 89–104. See also G. Pechey, 'Post-apartheid Narratives', in *Colonial Discourse/ Postcolonial Theory*, eds F. Barker, P. Hulme, & M. Iverson (Manchester & New York: Manchester University Press, 1994), pp. 151–171.

27 E. Mphahlele, quoted in P. Limb, 'Early ANC Leaders and the British World: Ambiguities and Identities', *Historia* 47.1 (2002): 56–82, p. 60.

28 See Green, 'Translating the Nation', p. 327.

29 Pechey, 'Post-apartheid Narratives', p. 158.

30 Matlwa, *Coconut*, pp. 188, 189.

31 Matlwa, *Coconut*, p. 189.

32 Duncan, *Lovedale*.

33 M. Sanders, *Complicities: The Intellectual and Apartheid* (Pietermaritzburg: UKZN Press, 2002), p. 108; see De Kock, *Civilising Barbarians*, and 'Sitting for the Civilization Test', pp. 396–397.

34 See, for example, P. Abrahams, *Tell Freedom* (London: Faber and Faber, 1954), pp. 161, 163–165, 235–236, 237–239, 255, 263. See also E. Mphahlele, *Down Second Avenue* (London: Faber and Faber, 1959), pp. 163–164, 178; and, for a scholarly assessment, C. Woeber, 'Error in the Religious Equation: Images of St Peter's School in South African Autobiography', *English Academy Review* 12 (1995): 58–69.

35 B. Modisane, *Blame Me on History* (Craighall: Ad. Donker, 1963; 1986), p. 218.

36 Duncan, *Lovedale*, p. 359. De Kock also writes about Lovedale as representative of the functioning of the mission schools, since it was 'the largest and most influential missionary educational institution in the country' (*Civilising Barbarians*, p. 69) well into the first half of the twentieth century.

37 B. Ashcroft, *Post-colonial Transformation* (London & New York: Routledge, 2001), p. 57. The term 'comprador' has been used by K.A. Appiah and Ngugi wa Thiong'o, amongst others.

38 As Homi Bhabha's work has illustrated. See H. Bhabha, *The Location of Culture* (London & New York: Routledge, 1994).

39 De Kock, 'Sitting for the Civilization Test,' pp. 396–397.

40 B. Peterson, 'Sol Plaatje's *Native Life in South Africa*: Melancholy Narratives, Petitioning Selves and the Ethics of Suffering', *The Journal of Commonwealth Literature* 43 (2008): 79–95, p. 80. Laura Chrisman calls for a new way of theorising black modernity, using Plaatje's work specifically as the example (L. Chrisman, 'Rethinking Black Atlanticism', *Black Scholar* 30.3/4 [Fall/Winter 2000]: 12–18).

41 See P. Limb, 'Early ANC Leaders'; D. Seddon, 'Shakespeare's Orality: Solomon Plaatje's Setswana Translations', *English Studies in Africa* 47.2 (2004): 77–95; De Kock, *Civilising Barbarians*; D. Attwell, *Rewriting Modernity*; D. Chanaiwa, 'African Humanism in Southern Africa: The Utopian, Traditionalist, and Colonialist

Worlds of Mission-Educated Elites', in *Independence Without Freedom: The Political Economy of Colonial Education in Southern Africa*, eds A.T. Mugomba & M. Nyaggah (Oxford & Santa Barbara, CA: ABC-Clio, 1980), pp. 9–39.

42 For an extended summary of Plaatje's life and works, see B. Willan, ed., *Sol Plaatje: Selected Writings* (Johannesburg: Wits University Press, 1996). The details of Plaatje's life provided here come from Willan's text.

43 See E. Boehmer, *Empire, the National, and the Postcolonial, 1890–1920* (Oxford: Oxford University Press, 2002).

44 Green, 'Translating the Nation', p. 327.

45 Boehmer, *Empire*, p. 126 (emphasis in the original). See also Green, 'Translating the Nation'.

46 Seddon, 'Shakespeare's Orality', p. 82.

47 Boehmer, *Empire*.

48 Boehmer, *Empire*, p. 134.

49 Boehmer, *Empire*, pp. 131–150. See also P. Limb, 'Sol Plaatje Reconsidered: Rethinking Plaatje's Attitudes to Class, Nation, Gender, and Empire', *African Studies* 62.1 (2003): 33–52, for more on Plaatje's complex position with regards to the empire he both embraced and critiqued.

50 Boehmer, *Empire*, p. 137.

51 Boehmer, *Empire*, p. 138.

52 T. Couzens, 'A Moment in the Past: William Tsikinya-Chaka', *Shakespeare in Southern Africa* 2 (1988): 60–66.

53 For an example of the former, see T. Couzens, *The New African: A Study of the Life and Works of H.I.E. Dhlomo* (Johannesburg: Ravan Press, 1985), pp. 6–18. For the latter, see D. Johnson, *Shakespeare and South Africa* (Oxford: Clarendon Press, 1996), pp. 74–110.

54 S. Plaatje, *Mhudi*, ed. T. Couzens (Broadway: Quagga, 1975). See D. Seddon, 'Shakespeare's Orality'.

55 See D. Schalkwyk & L. Lapula, 'Solomon Plaatje, William Shakespeare, and the Translations of Culture', *Pretexts: Literary and Cultural Studies* 9.1 (2000): 9–26, p. 13. This is a tactic employed

also by Bloke Modisane. See Distiller, *South Africa, Shakespeare, and Post-colonial Culture*, pp. 162–168.

56 C. Kahn, 'Remembering Shakespeare Imperially: The 1916 Tercentenary', *Shakespeare Quarterly* 52.4 (2001): 456–478, p. 457.

57 Kahn, 'Remembering Shakespeare Imperially', p. 462.

58 Kahn, 'Remembering Shakespeare Imperially', p. 475.

59 Kahn, 'Remembering Shakespeare Imperially', p. 475.

60 Willan, ed., *Sol Plaatje: Selected Writings*, p. 211.

61 Willan, ed., *Sol Plaatje: Selected Writings*, p. 212.

62 Seddon, 'Shakespeare's Orality,' p. 90.

63 D. Schalkwyk, 'Portrait and Proxy: Representing Plaatje and Plaatje Represented', *Scrutiny 2* 4.2 (1999): 14–29. See also Peterson, 'Sol Plaatje's *Native Life*', for an analysis of Plaatje's mode of address in *Native Life in South Africa*.

64 Willan, ed., *Sol Plaatje: Selected Writings*, p. 212.

65 Seddon, 'Shakespeare's Orality', p. 79.

66 Willan, ed., *Sol Plaatje: Selected Writings*, p. 211.

67 Green, 'Translating the Nation', p. 329.

68 Matlwa, *Coconut*, p. 126. Italics in the original.

69 See Chanaiwa, 'African Humanism in Southern Africa'.

CHAPTER 2 **'Through Shakespeare's Africa': 'Terror and murder'?**

1 A full analysis of this production is provided in the next chapter.

2 A. Sampson, *Drum: A Venture into the New Africa* (London: Collins, 1956); P. Gready, 'The Sophiatown Writers of the Fifties: The Unreal Reality of Their World', *Journal of Southern African Studies* 16.1 (1990): 139–164; D. Driver, '*Drum* Magazine (1951–59) and the Spatial Configurations of Gender', in *Text, Theory, Space: Land, Literature and History in South Africa and Australia*, eds K. Darian-Smith, L. Gunner, & S. Nuttall (London: Routledge, 1996), pp. 231–241.

3 For a full discussion of which see N. Distiller, *South Africa, Shakespeare and Post-colonial Culture* (Lampeter: Edmin Mellen, 2005), pp. 162–168.

4 M. Nicol, *A Good-looking Corpse* (London: Secker & Warburg, 1991), p. 26.

5 P. Stein & R. Jacobson, eds, *Sophiatown Speaks* (Johannesburg: Bertrams Avenue, 1986), p. 43.

6 Sampson, *Drum: A Venture*, p. 80.

7 Gready, 'Sophiatown Writers', p. 42.

8 For a discussion of Macbeth in this context, see N. Distiller, '"The Zulu Macbeth": The Value of an "African Shakespeare"', *Shakespeare Survey* 57 (2004): 159–168.

9 The following discussion of the *Drum* writers draws on N. Distiller, *South Africa, Shakespeare, and Post-colonial Culture*, ch. 4.

10 W. Soyinka, 'Shakespeare and the Living Dramatist', in *Art, Dialogue and Outrage: Essays on Literature and Culture* (Ibadan: New Horn Press, 1988). Soyinka suggests that Shakespeare must have been African, since in *Antony and Cleopatra* he understood Egypt so well.

11 C. Themba, 'Through Shakespeare's Africa', *New African* 2.8 (1963): 150–154, p. 150.

12 Themba, 'Through Shakespeare's Africa', p. 150

13 Themba, 'Through Shakespeare's Africa', p. 150.

14 Themba, 'Through Shakespeare's Africa', pp. 150–151.

15 Themba, 'Through Shakespeare's Africa', p. 154.

16 Themba, 'Through Shakespeare's Africa', p. 153.

17 Themba, 'Through Shakespeare's Africa', p. 153.

18 Themba, 'Through Shakespeare's Africa', p. 153.

19 Themba, 'Through Shakespeare's Africa', p. 153.

20 Themba, 'Through Shakespeare's Africa', p. 153.

21 Themba, 'Through Shakespeare's Africa', p. 154.

22 Themba, 'Through Shakespeare's Africa', p. 154.

23 This is not to excuse the sexism, which must be read in the context of the misogyny of 1950s *Drum* writing in general. The issue of a wounded masculinity comes up again in Modisane's writing, as will be discussed shortly.

24 In B. Peterson, *Monarchs, Missionaries and African Intellectuals: African Theatre and the Unmaking of Colonial Marginality* (Johannesburg: Wits University Press, 2000), p. 21.

25 B. Modisane, *Blame Me on History* (Craighall: Ad. Donker, 1963; 1986).

26 Modisane, *Blame Me*, pp. 179, 204, 302.

27 Modisane, *Blame Me*, p. 178

28 Modisane, *Blame Me*, p. 179.

29 Modisane, *Blame Me*, p. 143

30 Modisane, *Blame Me*, p. 231.

31 Modisane, *Blame Me*, p. 231.

32 Modisane, *Blame Me*, pp. 167–168.

33 M. Yogev, 'How Shall We Find the Concord of this Discord? Teaching Shakespeare in Israel, 1994', *Shakespeare Quarterly* 46.1 (1995): 157–164, p. 164.

34 M.J. Collins, 'For World and Stage: An Approach to Teaching Shakespeare', *Shakespeare Quarterly* 41.2 (1990): 251–261, especially p. 259.

35 J. Holmes, '"A World Elsewhere": Shakespeare in South Africa', *Shakespeare Survey* 55 (2002): 271–284.

36 Holmes, '"A World Elsewhere"', p. 278.

37 Holmes, '"A World Elsewhere"', p. 278.

38 This is a good example of the point made by Jonathan Dollimore about universal humanism's propensity to mystify suffering and ignore the historical causes of social inequality (J. Dollimore, *Radical Tragedy*, 2nd edition. [Hertfordshire: Harvester Wheatsheaf, 1989]).

39 S. Biko, *I Write What I Like*, ed. A. Stubbs (London: Bowerdean, 1978).

40 P.B. Rich, *White Power and the Liberal Conscience: Racial Segregation and South African Liberalism, 1921–60* (Manchester: Manchester University Press, 1984); J. Butler, R. Elphick, & D. Welsh, *Democratic Liberalism in South Africa: Its History and Prospects* (Middletown, CT, & Cape Town: Wesleyan University Press & David Philip, 1987); L. Husemeyer, ed., *Watchdogs or Hypocrites? The Amazing Debate on South African Liberals and Liberalism* (Johannesburg: Friedrich-Naumann-Stiftung, 1997); R.W. Johnson & D. Welsh, eds, *Ironic Victory: Liberalism in Post-liberation South Africa* (Oxford: Oxford University Press, 1998).

41 M. Orkin, *Shakespeare Against Apartheid* (Craighall: Ad. Donker, 1987).

42 A sustained discussion of this production of *The Tempest*, directed by Janice Honeyman and performed at the Baxter Theatre in Cape Town, is outside of the scope of this book, which ends with Thabo Mbeki's rule in 2008, as will be discussed in the last chapter. Briefly, however, in my opinion Honeyman's *Tempest*, while containing many powerful and beautiful moments, is typically guilty of using an ersatz Africanness to decorate a Shakespearean authority. As such it can be related to many of the criticisms made here. Nevertheless it was an infinitely more successful and better production than Sher and Doran's *Titus*. For a sustained analysis of Honeyman's *Tempest*, see S. Young, '"Let Your Indulgence Set Me Free": Reflections on an "Africanised" *Tempest* and its Implications for Critical Practice', *Social Dynamics* 36.2 (June 2010): 315–327.

43 A. Sher & G. Doran, *Woza Shakespeare! 'Titus Andronicus' in South Africa* (London: Methuen, 1996), p. 5.

44 Sher & Doran, *Woza Shakespeare!*, p. 19; emphasis in the original.

45 A. Sher, *The Feast* (London: Little, Brown, 1998).

46 Sher & Doran, *Woza Shakespeare!*, p. 138.

47 See P. Mullineux, 'An Examination of the Use of the Contextual Question in Examining Shakespeare's Plays at the Standard Ten Level in Cape Education Department Schools', MA diss., Rhodes University, 1988; P.S. Walters & V. England, *The Teaching of English Literature in Black High Schools* (Grahamstown: ISEA, Rhodes

University, 1988); P. Lenahan, 'Interacting with Shakespeare's Figurative Language: A Project in Materials Development for the L2 Classroom', MA diss., Rhodes University, 1994; A. Coetzee, 'Justifying the Teaching of Shakespeare to ESL Learners in the Junior Secondary Phase', MA diss., University of Potchefstroom, 1997. See also M. Kirkwood, 'The Colonizer: A Critique of the English South African Culture Theory', in *Poetry South Africa: Selected Papers from 'Poetry 74'*, eds P. Wilhelm & J.A. Polley (Craighall: Ad. Donker, 1976), pp. 102–133.

CHAPTER 3 Tony's Will: *Titus Andronicus* in South Africa, 1995

1 Quoted in J. Bate, 'Introduction', in *Titus Andronicus*, ed. J. Bate (London & New York: Routledge, 1995), pp. 1–121; p. 33.

2 Quoted in H.G. Metz, 'Stage History of *Titus Andronicus*', *Shakespeare Quarterly* 28.2 (1997): 154–169, p. 157.

3 Quoted in Bate, 'Introduction', p. 34.

4 Quoted in M.E. Smith, 'Spectacles of Torment in *Titus Andronicus*', *SEL* 36 (1996): 315–331, p. 315.

5 Quoted in Bate, 'Introduction', p. 11.

6 Metz, 'Stage History', p. 154. See also Bate, 'Introduction', pp. 1, 34; A.C. Dessen, *Titus Andronicus* (Manchester & New York: Manchester University Press, 1989).

7 The extent of the play's violence has been the subject of much critical commentary. For example, see R.A. Foakes, *Shakespeare and Violence* (Cambridge: Cambridge University Press, 2003), p. 56.

8 Metz, 'Stage History', pp. 159, 165.

9 Metz, 'Stage History', p. 167; R. Quince, *Shakespeare in South Africa: Stage Productions During the Apartheid Era* (New York: Peter Lang, 2000), pp. 34–36. Metz seems unaware of Sher and Doran's production.

10 A. Sher & G. Doran, *Woza Shakespeare! 'Titus Andronicus' in South Africa* (London: Methuen, 1996), p. 15.

11 Sher & Doran, *Woza Shakespeare!*, p. 25.

12 Sher & Doran, *Woza Shakespeare!*, p. 25.

13 Sher & Doran, *Woza Shakespeare!*, p. 150.

14 Sher & Doran, *Woza Shakespeare!*, p. 15.

15 Sher & Doran, *Woza Shakespeare!*, p. 45.

16 Sher & Doran, *Woza Shakespeare!*, p. 45.

17 Sher & Doran, *Woza Shakespeare!*, p. 117.

18 Sher & Doran, *Woza Shakespeare!*, p. 11.

19 Sher & Doran, *Woza Shakespeare!*, p. 67.

20 Sher & Doran, *Woza Shakespeare!*, p. 167.

21 The oppositional relationship is developed also by the descriptions of place in the book. From the book's opening, there is an implicit comparison in the description of the 'English' and the 'South African'. This binary is suggested in the initial description of Sher's wait outside South Africa House, to vote in the country's first democratic elections. He moves 'through brilliant South African-type sunshine on one side, cool English spring shade on the other' (Sher & Doran, *Woza Shakespeare!*, p. 4). South Africa House contains 'the provincial (dusty dioramas of South African scenes)' (Sher & Doran, *Woza Shakespeare!*, p. 4). Why dioramas of South African scenes are provincial, and the diorama he and Doran have in their house, of Elizabethan London, is romantic (Sher & Doran, *Woza Shakespeare!*, p. 68), points to the different ways in which these two landscapes are inflected. Similarly, Johannesburg is 'a harsh urban jungle … [T]he place seems full of Aarons – people whose capacity for violence stems sometimes from the need to survive, sometimes because they've forgotten any other way' (Sher & Doran, *Woza Shakespeare!*, p. 156). In contrast, London 'does make me [Sher] feel calm and well' (Sher & Doran, *Woza Shakespeare!*, p. 270) and has 'all this transport, this easy, *safe* transport!' (Sher & Doran, *Woza Shakespeare!*, p. 299).

22 Sher & Doran, *Woza Shakespeare!*, p. 13.

23 Sher & Doran, *Woza Shakespeare!*, p. 13.

24 Sher & Doran, *Woza Shakespeare!*, p. 124.

25 The designation 'coloured' is a colonial and then apartheid category,
eventually designating a group of people with its own cultural
markers and identities. It is a contested and fraught label, raising as
it can the artificiality of the project of racial separation (N. Distiller
& M. Samuelson, '"Denying the Coloured Mother": Gender and
Race in South Africa', *L'Homme* 16.2 [2005]: 28–46). Sher and Doran
explain the specifically South African meaning to their audience in
a staged dialogue:

> 'Coloured means specifically mixed race, doesn't it?' I say to
> Tony. 'Not Indian, not white, not black [the three other main
> apartheid racial classifications], mixed race.'
>
> 'Yes,' says Tony. 'Coffee-coloured. Surely you knew that?'
> 'Of course,' I snap defensively. 'Just checking.' (Sher &
> Doran, *Woza Shakespeare!*, p. 42)

26 See S. Dubow, *Racial Segregation and the Origins of Apartheid in
South Africa, 1919–36* (London: Macmillan, 1989).

27 British critic Michael Kustow (of whose review says the man who
refers to the South African critics whose reviews he doesn't like as
'Digby Wigby' and 'Mark Ge-vicious', 'At last, a grown-up view of
what we've done' [Sher & Doran, *Woza Shakespeare!*, p. 208]) relays
the response to Sher's accent of one audience member, 'a rich-
looking white man': '"I think they're trying to make fools of us," he
growls.' The accusation implicit in the description of the man (one
wonders what exactly 'rich-looking' is) helps to frame his response
as a kind of provincial snobbery.

28 See E. Hees, review of *Woza Shakespeare! 'Titus Andronicus' in South
Africa*, by A. Sher & G. Doran, *South African Theatre Journal* 1 & 2
(1997): 298–304, p. 302.

29 Sher & Doran, *Woza Shakespeare!*, pp. 3–4.

30 Sher & Doran, *Woza Shakespeare!*, p. 17.

31 Sher & Doran, *Woza Shakespeare!*, pp. 15, 17.

32 A. Sher, *Beside Myself: An Autobiography* (London: Hutchinson,
2000), p. 262.

33 Sher, *Beside Myself*, p. 265.

34 Sher & Doran, *Woza Shakespeare!*, p. 254.

35 Sher & Doran, *Woza Shakespeare!*, pp. 211–212.

36 Sher & Doran, *Woza Shakespeare!*, p. 221.

37 Sher & Doran, *Woza Shakespeare!*, pp. ix–x.

38 Sher & Doran, *Woza Shakespeare!*, p. 11. There are also scripted 'exchanges', resulting in a strained realism, through which the presentation of clichéd South Africanisms are explained to the reader:

> 'The hadedahs are calling ... ' says Dan.
> "The what?"
> "The hadedahs, they're ibis, they're called hadedahs because that's what they cry." And someone does an impression ...
> (Sher & Doran, *Woza Shakespeare!*, p. 122)

39 Sher & Doran, *Woza Shakespeare!*, p. 218.

40 Sher & Doran, *Woza Shakespeare!*, p. 213.

41 Sher & Doran, *Woza Shakespeare!*, pp. 154, 230.

42 S. Gray, 'Not a Sher-fire Hit', *Mail & Guardian Online* 10 January 1997. Accessed January 2008, http://www.chico.mweb.co.za/mg/art/reviews/97jan/12jan-sher.html.

43 Sher & Doran, *Woza Shakespeare!*, p. 160.

44 Hees, Review, p. 301.

45 Sher & Doran, *Woza Shakespeare!*, p. 116.

46 Sher & Doran, *Woza Shakespeare!*, p. 117.

47 H. Bernstein, *The Rift: The Exile Experiences of South Africans* (London: Jonathan Cape, 1994), p. 359.

48 Sher & Doran, *Woza Shakespeare!*, p. 38.

49 Sher & Doran, *Woza Shakespeare!*, p. 111.

50 Sher & Doran, *Woza Shakespeare!*, p. 199.

51 Sher & Doran, *Woza Shakespeare!*, p. 243.

52 C. Achebe, 'An Image of Africa: Racism in Conrad's *Heart of Darkness*', in *Heart of Darkness: An Authoritative Text, Background, and Sources, Criticism*, 3rd edition, ed. R. Kimbrough (London: Norton, 1988), pp. 251–261.

53 *Titus*, as some critics noticed (T. Howard, review of *Wozza* [sic] *Shakespeare! 'Titus Andronicus' in South Africa*, *New Theatre Quaterly* 14.3 [1998]: 294), is a play remarkably ill-suited to a reconciliatory message, even with the amended ending. It stages the failure of language to understand pain and torture, the impossibility of separating the barbaric from the civilised, the misogyny which drives a state predicated on patriarchal family values; its revenge tragedy imperatives glory in gory predeterminism. Furthermore, if one wants to read the play as a warning, Sher and Doran's production, because of its reliance on confusing racial stereotypes (ideological, physical, and aural), is able to only improperly realise this potential.

54 Sher & Doran, *Woza Shakespeare!*, p. 48.

55 Sher & Doran, *Woza Shakespeare!*, p. 229.

56 Sher & Doran, *Woza Shakespeare!*, pp. 52, 256.

57 Sher & Doran, *Woza Shakespeare!*, p. 174.

58 Sher & Doran, *Woza Shakespeare!*, p. 42.

59 Sher & Doran, *Woza Shakespeare!*, p. 42.

60 Sher & Doran, *Woza Shakespeare!*, p. 42.

61 Sher & Doran, *Woza Shakespeare!*, p. 52.

62 See Chris Thurman's comments in this regard, and in relation to the casting of the nurse as a 'maid'. C. Thurman, 'Sher and Doran's *Titus Andronicus* (1995): Importing Shakespeare, Exporting South Africa', *Shakespeare in Southern Africa* 18 (2006): 29–36, p. 32.

63 A. Haupt, 'Identity and the Politics of Representation in Hip Hop', in *Under Construction: 'Race' and Identity in South Africa Today*, eds N. Distiller & M. Steyn (Cape Town: Heinemann, 2004), pp. 199–209, especially pp. 202–203.

64 Sher & Doran, *Woza Shakespeare!*, p. 47.

65 Sher & Doran, *Woza Shakespeare!*, p. 77.

66 Sher & Doran, *Woza Shakespeare!*, p. 147.

67 Sher & Doran, *Woza Shakespeare!*, p. 147.

68 Sher & Doran, *Woza Shakespeare!*, p. 126.

69 This is a reference to strikes in response to the apartheid 'homeland' Bophuthatswana government's initial decision not to participate in South Africa's first democratic elections in 1994. South African right-wing extremists invaded the homeland in support of its government, thus fuelling the tensions which culminated in riots and looting.

70 Sher & Doran, *Woza Shakespeare!*, p. 113. The inclusion in Sher's autobiography, *Beside Myself*, of a similar discussion amongst his family members (p. 257) again raises the question of the shaping of events to the demands of a script. In itself, this is the prerogative of the writer, of course. In the context of a certain use of 'South Africa' as both a territory and an ideological space for the working out of identity issues, especially in the highly politicised and moralised critique of the country that emerges from Sher's experience of staging *Titus* here, the invocation of 'fact' becomes open to more sustained scrutiny.

71 Sher & Doran, *Woza Shakespeare!*, p. 113.

72 Sher & Doran, *Woza Shakespeare!*, p. 114.

73 Sher & Doran, *Woza Shakespeare!*, p. 110.

74 Sher & Doran, *Woza Shakespeare!*, p. 279.

75 Sher & Doran, *Woza Shakespeare!*, p. 179.

76 D. Willis, '"This Gnawing Vulture": Revenge, Trauma Theory, and *Titus Andronicus*', *Shakespeare Quarterly* 53.1 (2002): 21–52.

77 L. Noble, '"And Make Two Pasties of Your Shameful Heads": Medicinal Cannibalism and Healing the Body Politic in *Titus Andronicus*', *English Literary History* 70 (2003): 677–708, p. 688.

78 Noble, '"And Make Two Pasties"', pp. 688–689.

79 Willis, '"This Gnawing Vulture"'; B.A. Mowat, 'Lavinia's Message: Shakespeare and Myth', *Renaissance Papers* (1981): 55–69; C. Marshall, '"I Can Interpret All Her Martyr'd Signs": *Titus Andronicus*, Feminism, and the Limits of Interpretation', in *Sexuality and Politics in Renaissance Drama*, eds C. Levin & K. Robertson (Lampeter: Edwin Mellen, 1991), pp. 193–214; B. Harris, 'Sexuality as a Signifier for Power Relations: Using Lavinia, of Shakespeare's *Titus Andronicus*', *Criticism* 38.3 (1996): 383–407.

80 Marshall, '"I Can Interpret"', p. 208.

81 Sher & Doran, *Woza Shakespeare!*, p. 51.

82 See Z. Erasmus, ed., *Coloured by History, Shaped by Place: New Perspectives on Coloured Identities in Cape Town* (Cape Town: Kwela & South African History Online, 2001). Francesca Royster has written about the play's use of whiteness. For her, Tamora has to be 'hyperwhite' ('White-Limed Walls: Whiteness and Gothic Extremism in Shakespeare's *Titus Andronicus*', *Shakespeare Quarterly* 51.4 (2000): 432–455, p. 432) in order for the play to be seen to interrogate whiteness, and thus to explore 'the stranger ... from within' (p. 434), amongst other issues.

83 Sher & Doran, *Woza Shakespeare!*, p. 50.

84 Sher & Doran, *Woza Shakespeare!*, p. 177.

85 V.M. Vaughan, 'The Construction of Barbarism in *Titus Andronicus*', in *Race, Ethnicity, and Power in the Renaissance*, ed. J.G. MacDonald (Madison, NJ, & London: Associated University Presses, 1997), pp. 165–180; Smith, 'Spectacles'.

86 H. James, 'Cultural Disintegration in *Titus Andronicus*: Mutilating Titus, Vergil, and Rome', in *Violence in Drama*, ed. J.M.A. Redmond (Cambridge & New York: Cambridge University Press, 1991), pp. 123–140.

87 A. Sher, *The Feast* (London: Little, Brown, 1998).

88 See M. Steyn, *Whiteness Just Isn't What It Used To Be: White Identity in a Changing South Africa* (Albany: State University of New York Press, 2001).

89 Sher, *Beside Myself*, pp. 264–265.

90 D. Ricci, 'Titus Topples into the "Relevant" Pit', *Shakespeare in Southern Africa* 8 (1995): 81–82, p. 82.

91 Sher & Doran, *Woza Shakespeare!*, p. 261.

92 Sher & Doran, *Woza Shakespeare!*, p. 205.

93 Sher & Doran, *Woza Shakespeare!*, p. 207.

94 Sher & Doran, *Woza Shakespeare!*, p. 272.

95 Sher & Doran, *Woza Shakespeare!*, p. 205.

96 Sher & Doran, *Woza Shakespeare!*, p. 206.

97 Sher & Doran, *Woza Shakespeare!*, p. 208.

98 Sher & Doran, *Woza Shakespeare!*, p. 34.

CHAPTER 4 Begging the questions: Producing Shakespeare for post-apartheid South African schools

1 He echoes a sentence in the book when he writes, 'After all, where will Setswana get you?' (Matlwa wrote, '*What has Sepedi ever done for them?*' as we saw in chapter one). This may reflect the catchphrase quality of the sentiment, or it may indicate that he is using the book as a springboard for the article. He concludes his article: 'if truth be told, they thrive because they are what we all want to be'. This also echoes sentiments in the book, particularly a scene between Fikile and the 'coconut kid' Ayanda. This scene is referenced in the final chapter of this book.

2 A. Mngxitama, 'Coconut Kids Have Lost Touch with Their Roots', *City Press* 30 September 2007, p. 26.

3 See, for example, A. Sinfield, 'Give an Account of Shakespeare and Education, Showing Why You Think They are Effective and What You Have Appreciated about Them. Support Your Comments with Precise References', in *Political Shakespeare: New Essays in Cultural Materialism*, eds J. Dollimore & A. Sinfield (Manchester & New York: Manchester University Press, 1985), pp. 134–157; M. Orkin, *Shakespeare Against Apartheid* (Craighall: Ad. Donker, 1987).

4 See Orkin, *Shakespeare Against Apartheid*; M. Orkin, 'The Politics of Editing the Shakespeare Text in South Africa', *Current Writing* 5.1 (1993): 48–59.

5 See, in addition, M. Orkin, 'Shakespeare and the Politics of "Unrest"', *English Academy Review* 8 (1991): 85–97; M. Orkin, 'Representing *The Tempest* in South Africa (1955–90)', *Shakespeare in Southern Africa* 6 (1993): 45–60; M. Orkin, 'Possessing the Book and Peopling the Text', in *Post-colonial Shakespeares*, eds A. Loomba & M. Orkin (London & New York: Routledge, 1998), pp. 186–204; M. Orkin, 'Whose *Muti* in the Web of It? Seeking "Post"-colonial Shakespeare', *Journal of Commonwealth Literature* 33.2 (1998): 15–37; D. Johnson, 'Starting Positions: The Social Functions of Literature

in the Cape', *Journal of Southern African Studies* 19.4 (1993): 615–633; D. Johnson, 'From the Colonial to the Post-colonial: Shakespeare and Education in Africa', in *Post-colonial Shakespeares*, eds A. Loomba & M. Orkin (London & New York: Routledge, 1998), pp. 218–234; D. Johnson, 'Lessons from Africa', *Mail & Guardian* Beyond Matric Supplement, 7 September 2001, pp. 21–27.

6   See chapter 5 in N. Distiller, *South Africa, Shakespeare, and Post-colonial Culture* (Lampeter: Edwin Mellen, 2005).

7   See, for example, G. Taylor, *Reinventing Shakespeare: A Cultural History from the Restoration to the Present* (Oxford: Oxford University Press, 1989).

8   G. Holderness, ed., *The Shakespeare Myth* (New York: Manchester University Press, 1988).

9   S.A. Beehler, '"That's a Certain Text": Problematizing Shakespeare Instruction in American Schools and Colleges', *Shakespeare Quarterly* 41.2 (1990): 195–205; P. O'Brien, 'Doing Shakespeare: "Yo! A Hit! A Very Palpable Hit!"', *English Journal* 82.4 (1993): 40–45.

10 According to Nigel Bakker at the Education Department of the University of Cape Town, and one of the editors of the Maskew Miller Longman Shakespeare discussed in this chapter (personal correspondence, May 2011).

11 R.E. Salomone & J.E. Davis, eds, *Teaching Shakespeare into the Twenty-first Century* (Athens: Ohio University Press, 1997), p. xii.

12 M. Gilmour, ed., *Shakespeare for All in Secondary Schools* (London: Cassell, 1996).

13 A.A. Makua, 'Taking the Fear out of Shakespeare: Approaches to the Teaching of *Macbeth*', *Educamus* (July 1989): 18–20, p. 18.

14 The study of English literature during apartheid was a complex enterprise for most South African learners. Questions were often raised about what literature was appropriate for black South African children, which was related to questions about what literature teaching could and should accomplish. Answers varied according to the political starting point of researchers, from the worst kind of conservatively Christianised 'liberalism' (P. Mullineux, 'An Examination of the Use of the Contextual Question in Examining Shakespeare's Plays at the Standard Ten Level in Cape Education

Department Schools', MA diss., Rhodes University, 1988;
A. Coetzee, 'Justifying the Teaching of Shakespeare to ESL
Learners in the Junior Secondary Phase', MA diss., University
of Potchefstroom, 1997), to more sensible attempts to review the
arguments and to engage with some of the complexities of the South
African situation (P.S. Walters & V. England, *The Teaching of English
Literature in Black High Schools* [Grahamstown: ISEA, Rhodes
University, 1988]; P. Lenahan, 'Interacting with Shakespeare's
Figurative Language: A Project in Materials Development for the L2
Classroom', MA diss., Rhodes University, 1994).

15 A. Lemmer, 'Upgrading the Study of Shakespeare in Southern
African Secondary Schools: An Interim Report on the Schools' Text
Project', *Shakespeare in Southern Africa* 2 (1988): 67–77, p. 69.

16 Distiller, *South Africa, Shakespeare, and Post-colonial Culture*,
pp. 231–232.

17 A. Lemmer & J. Bursey, Introductory material to *Shakespeare's
'Macbeth'* (Manzini: Macmillan, 1994), p. 4.

18 Lemmer & Bursey, Introductory material, p. 7.

19 N. Distiller, '"The Zulu Macbeth": the Value of an "African
Shakespeare"', *Shakespeare Survey* 57 (2004): 159–168.

20 Lemmer & Bursey, Introductory material, p. 7.

21 T. Eagleton, 'The Witches are the Heroines of the Piece...', in
'Macbeth': Contemporary Critical Essays, ed. A. Sinfield (London:
Macmillan, 1992), pp. 46–52.

22 Lemmer & Bursey, Introductory material, p. 8.

23 A. Sinfield, '*Macbeth*: History, Ideology and Intellectuals', in
'Macbeth': Contemporary Critical Essays, ed. A. Sinfield (London:
Macmillan, 1992), pp. 121–136.

24 Lemmer & Bursey, Introductory material, p. 28.

25 Lemmer & Bursey, Introductory material, p. 30.

26 W. Shakespeare, *Macbeth*, ed. N. Bakker, B. Mosala, A. Parr & L.
Singh (Cape Town: Maskew Miller Longman, 1996).

27 Shakespeare, *Macbeth*, Maskew Miller Longman, p. 24.

28 Shakespeare, *Macbeth* , Maskew Miller Longman, pp. 120–121.

29 Distiller, *South Africa, Shakespeare, and Post-colonial Culture*, p. 241.

30 Lemmer, 'Upgrading the Study', p. 69; Distiller, *South Africa, Shakespeare, and Post-colonial Culture*, p. 230.

31 W. Saunders, 'Mastering English', *Reality* (March/April 1992): 15–16; J. Paton, 'A Pleasurable Pathway to the Works of Shakespeare', *The Daily News* 25 February 1993, p. 23.

32 'Comments on the Series', Shakespeare 2000 website, n.d. Accessed April 2005, http://www.shakespeare2000.com/comments.html.

33 'Comments on the Series'.

34 W. Saunders, *Shakespeare's 'Macbeth' in Modern English* (Parklands: Shakespeare 2000/Jacklin, 2001), p. 2.

35 Saunders, *Shakespeare's 'Macbeth'*, pp. 1–2.

36 I. ii. 10–12.

37 From I. ii. 6–7.

38 Saunders, *Shakespeare's 'Macbeth'*, p. 194.

39 Saunders, *Shakespeare's 'Macbeth'*, p. 12.

40 For example, M. de Grazia, *Shakespeare Verbatim: The Reproduction of Authenticity and the 1790 Apparatus* (Oxford: Clarendon Press, 1991); M. de Grazia & P. Stallybrass, 'The Materiality of the Shakespearean Text', *Shakespeare Quarterly* 44.3 (1993): 255–283; L. Marcus, *Unediting the Renaissance: Shakespeare, Marlowe, Milton* (London & New York: Routledge, 1996); D. Scott Kastan, *Shakespeare and the Book* (Cambridge: Cambridge University Press, 2001).

41 Saunders, *Shakespeare's 'Macbeth'*, p. 3.

42 Saunders, *Shakespeare's 'Macbeth'*, p. 11.

43 Saunders, *Shakespeare's 'Macbeth'*, p. 5.

44 'Matric', the final year of high school, is, under the post-apartheid education system, called Grade 12. The language of this comment may date it. Equally it may indicate that the intended recipients – prospective purchasers – are not current students.

45 'Comments on the Series'.

46 Paton, 'A Pleasurable Pathway'.

47 Sinfield, 'Give an Account'.

48 C. Belsey, *The Subject of Tragedy: Identity and Difference in Renaissance Drama* (London & New York: Methuen, 1985), p. 53; M.D. Bristol, *Shakespeare's America, America's Shakespeare* (London & New York: Routledge, 1990), p. 21.

49 Orkin, 'Politics of Editing', pp. 54, 57.

50 R. Cloud, '"The Very Names of the Persons": Editing and the Invention of Dramatick Character', in *Staging the Renaissance*, eds D. Scott Kastan & P. Stallybrass (New York & London: Routledge, 1991), pp. 88–96.

51 K. Cunningham, 'Shakespeare, the Public, and Public Education', *Shakespeare Quarterly* 49.3 (1998): 293–298, p. 295.

52 See M. Kirkwood, 'The Colonizer: A Critique of the English South African Culture Theory', in *Poetry South Africa: Selected Papers from Poetry 74*, eds P. Wilhelm & J.A. Polley (Craighall: Ad. Donker, 1976), pp. 102–133.

53 W. Shakespeare, *Macbeth*. Wits Schools Shakespeare edition, eds H. Davis, P. Farrands, & J. Parmenter (Cape Town: Nasou Via Afrika, 2007), p. 4.

54 Shakespeare, *Macbeth*, Wits, p. 4.

55 The other authors discussed are H.I.E. Dhlomo, Mbulelo Mzamane, and Ahmed Essop.

56 Shakespeare, *Macbeth*, Wits, p. 172.

57 Shakespeare, *Macbeth*, Wits, p. 173.

58 See Distiller, '"Zulu Macbeth"'.

59 Shakespeare, *Macbeth*, Wits, p. 6.

CHAPTER 5 English and the African Renaissance

1   S. Baldauf, 'Thabo Mbeki: The Fall of Africa's Shakespearean Figure', *Christian Science Monitor* 22 September 2008. Accessed 1 June 2011, http://www.csmonitor.com/World/Africa/2008/0922/p01s01-woaf.html.

2   P. Vale & S. Maseko, 'South Africa and the African Renaissance', in *South Africa and Africa: Reflections on the African Renaissance* (Braamfontein: Foundation for Global Dialogue Occasional Paper No. 17, October 1998), pp. 2–15; p. 4.

3   T. Mbeki, 'The African Renaissance', in *South Africa and Africa: Reflections on the African Renaissance* (Braamfontein: Foundation for Global Dialogue Occasional Paper No. 17, October 1998), pp. 38–41; p. 40.

4   V. Mavimbela, 'The African Renaissance: A Workable Dream', in *South Africa and Africa: Reflections on the African Renaissance* (Braamfontein: Foundation for Global Dialogue Occasional Paper No. 17, October 1998), pp. 29–34; p. 31.

5   Vale & Maseko, 'South Africa', p. 4.

6   C. Landsberg & F. Kornegay, 'The African Renaissance: A Quest for Pax Africana and Pan-Africanism', in *South Africa and Africa: Reflections on the African Renaissance* (Braamfontein: Foundation for Global Dialogue Occasional Paper No. 17, October 1998), pp. 16–28; p.17.

7   T. Mbeki, 'Prologue', in *African Renaissance: The New Struggle*, ed. M.W. Makgoba (Sandton & Cape Town: Mafube & Tafelberg, 1999), pp. xiii–xxi, p. xviii.

8   B.M. Magubane, 'The African Renaissance in Historical Perspective', in *African Renaissance: The New Struggle*, ed. M.W. Makgoba (Sandton & Cape Town: Mafube & Tafelberg, 1999), pp. 10–36.

9   Y. Dalamba, 'Towards an African Renaissance: Some Thoughts on the Renaissance Conference September 28th & 29th 1998 and its Future Implications', *Critical Arts* 14.1 (2000): 44–72, pp. 59–62; Vale & Maseko, 'South Africa', p. 10.

10 The proponents of the African Renaissance at the Johannesburg conference were careful to palliate such fears in the definition they offered of the 'African' who could partake of the promised Renaissance. An idealised, homogenised 'Africanness' was strategically invoked to exclude neither diasporic black Africans nor white South Africans (M.W. Makgoba, T. Shope, & T. Mazwai, 'Introduction', in *African Renaissance: The New Struggle*, ed. M.W. Makgoba [Sandton & Cape Town: Mafube & Tafelberg, 1999],

pp. i–xii; p. ix). Access to Africanness depends on a 'sincere' and 'life-long' commitment to the continent which is 'beneficial to the masses' (Dalamba, 'Towards an African Renaissance', p. 51) – a definition which avoids the problems of continental location and of 'racial' classification, but which brings other problems, such as quantification.

11 Vale & Maseko, 'South Africa', p. 12.

12 Meant here inclusively. In this regard I find Dalamba's identification of 'so-called "Coloureds"' as not as African as black Africans highly problematic (Dalamba, 'Towards an African Renaissance', p. 51).

13 K.G. Tomaselli, 'Cultural Studies and Renaissance in Africa: Recovering Praxis', *Scrutiny 2* 4.2 (1999): 43–48, p. 45.

14 Dalamba, 'Towards an African Renaissance', p. 45.

15 See also Mavimbela, 'The African Renaissance', p. 30.

16 Dalamba, 'Towards an African Renaissance', p. 67; see also H.W. Vilakazi, 'The African Renaissance', *New Agenda* 4 (2001): 56–67.

17 Magubane, 'The African Renaissance', pp. 13, 15, 17.

18 M. Mamdani, 'There Can Be No African Renaissance Without an Africa-focussed Intelligentsia', in *African Renaissance: The New Struggle*, ed. M.W. Makgoba (Sandton & Cape Town: Mafube & Tafelberg, 1999), pp. 125–134; p. 125.

19 Landsberg & Kornegay, 'The African Renaissance', p. 16.

20 Magubane, 'The African Renaissance', p. 21.

21 Dalamba, 'Towards an African Renaissance', p. 68.

22 A. Loomba, *Shakespeare, Race, and Colonialism* (Oxford: Oxford University Press, 2002).

23 M.G. Mugo, 'African Culture in Education for Sustainable Development', in *African Renaissance: The New Struggle*, ed. M.W. Makgoba (Sandton & Cape Town: Mafube & Tafelberg, 1999), pp. 210–232; p. 210; Vilakazi, 'The African Renaissance', pp. 56–57.

24 L. Marcus, 'Renaissance/Early Modern Studies', in *Redrawing the Boundaries: The Transformation of English and American Literary Studies*, eds S. Greenblatt & G. Gunn (New York: Modern Language Association of America, 1992), pp. 41–63; p. 61.

25 A.F. Kinney, 'Preface', in *Renaissance Historicism*, eds A.F. Kinney & D.S. Collins (Amherst: University of Massachusetts Press, 1987), pp. viii–xv; p. xiv. E.J. Bellamy, 'Psychoanalysis and the Subject in/of/for the Renaissance', in *Reconfiguring the Renaisance: Essays in Critical Materialism*, ed. J. Crewe (Lewisburg: Bucknell University Press, 1992), pp. 19–33; p. 19. J.E. Howard, 'The New Historicism in Renaissance Studies', in *Renaissance Historicism*, eds A.F. Kinney & D.S. Collins (Amherst: University of Massachusetts Press, 1987), pp. 3–33; p. 5. D. Bruster, 'Shakespeare and the End of History: Period as Brand Name', in *Shakespeare and Modernity*, ed. H. Grady (London: Routledge, 2000), pp. 168–188; p. 170.

26 H. White, *Tropics of Discourse: Essays in Cultural Criticism* (Baltimore & London: Johns Hopkins University Press, 1978), p. 44.

27 J. Burckhardt, *The Civilization of the Renaissance in Italy* (London: Phaidon, 1944), p. 82.

28 Burckhardt, *Civilization*, p. 104.

29 White, *Tropics of Discourse*, p. 53.

30 Mavimbela, 'The African Renaissance', p. 30.

31 Marcus, 'Renaissance/Early Modern Studies', p. 43.

32 Bruster, 'Shakespeare', p. 172.

33 Mamdani, 'There Can Be No African Renaissance'; Vale & Maseko, 'South Africa'.

34 Dalamba, 'Towards an African Renaissance', p. 46.

35 For example, Vilakazi, 'The African Renaissance', pp. 60–61.

36 T. Lodge, *Politics in South Africa from Mandela to Mbeki* (Cape Town: David Philip, 2002).

37 Marcus, 'Renaissance/Early Modern Studies', p. 43.

38 Lodge, *Politics in South Africa*, pp. 228, 230.

39 Vale & Maseko, 'South Africa', p. 8.

40 Vale & Maseko, 'South Africa', p. 8.

41 Vale & Maseko, 'South Africa', p. 9. And yet the African Renaissance was designed to work within globalisation; its developers had an

active awareness of the contingencies and demands of the global system when they put the concept into circulation. The African Renaissance as an economic framework (which drew its social and cultural legitimation from its metaphorical suggestiveness, in the context of Africa's traditional positioning within colonial discourses) was designed to capitalise on the world situation at the time; it targeted foreign investment, and sought to attract multinational corporations (Landsberg & Kornegay, 'The African Renaissance'; S.M. Cleary, 'African Renaissance: Challenges for South Africa', in *The African Renaissance: Occasional Papers* [Johannesburg: Konrad Adenauer Stiftung, 1998], pp. 21–27). In this is once more a marker of African modernity.

42 Post-colonialism has been accused of being a product of globalisation (E. San Juan, Jr, *Beyond Postcolonial Theory* [London: Macmillan, 1999]; A. Dirlik, 'The Postcolonial Aura: Third World Criticism in the Age of Global Capitalism', *Critical Inquiry* 20 [1994]: 328–356; K. Sole, 'South Africa Passes the Posts', *Alternation* 4.1 [1997]: 116–151) and I think there is much of value in this critique; however, here I use the label to designate a body of theory that, as part of its mandate, tries to identify and address neo-colonial realities, even as its most successful proponents have unprecedented access to the centres of cultural, academic, and economic power due to a relatively new class-based global mobility.

43 Mavimbela, 'The African Renaissance', pp. 29–30.

44 Mavimbela, 'The African Renaissance', p. 31.

45 Mavimbela, 'The African Renaissance', p. 33.

46 Vale & Maseko, 'South Africa', p. 9.

47 Mavimbela, 'The African Renaissance', p. 30.

48 Dalamba, 'Towards an African Renaissance', p. 50.

49 A. Amoko, 'The Magistrature of English: Postcolonialism, Globalism and Literary Studies', unpublished paper, 'Condition of the Subject' Conference, London, July 2003.

50 In addition, the fact that academia itself exists within the global marketplace in part accounts for the proliferation of innovative new approaches which have complicated the definition of Eng Lit (as noted by Greenblatt and Gunn [Stephen Greenblatt & Giles Gunn,

eds, *Redrawing the Boundaries: The Transformation of English and American Literary Studies* (New York: Modern Language Association of America, 1992)]). Academics are under pressure to produce the goods, and the Renaissance is a period whose literature is well suited to answer this need (J.E. Howard, 'The New Historicism', pp. 3–33; S. Fish, *Professional Correctness: Literary Studies and Political Change* [London & Cambridge, MA: Harvard University Press, 1995]).

51 Quoted in A.F. Kinney, 'Preface', p. viii.

52 Mavimbela, 'The African Renaissance', p. 31; see also Dalamba, 'Towards an African Renaissance'.

53 Greenblatt & Gunn, *Redrawing the Boundaries*.

54 Mbeki, 'The African Renaissance', p. 41.

55 See, for example, H. Grady, *Shakespeare's Universal Wolf: Studies in Early Modern Reification* (Oxford: Clarendon Press, 1996).

56 L. de Kock, 'English and the Colonisation of Form', *Journal of Literary Studies* 8.1 (June 1992): 33–54; G. Viswanathan, *Masks of Conquest: Literary Study and British Rule in India* (New York: Columbia University Press, 1989).

57 Vale & Maseko, 'South Africa', p. 13.

58 Vale & Maseko, 'South Africa', p. 14.

59 Mbeki, 'The African Renaissance'.

60 Vale & Maseko, 'South Africa', p. 6.

61 De Kock, 'English and the Colonisation of Form', p. 35.

62 De Kock, 'English and the Colonisation of Form', p. 39.

63 It is ironic, then, that even as its original proponents stress the importance of the traditional liberal arts in developing an educational, and thus a cultural, agenda in both Renaissances, European and African (Dalamba, 'Towards an African Renaissance', p. 45; P.P. Ntuli, 'The Missing Link between Culture and Education: Are We Still Chasing Gods that Are Not Our Own?' in *African Renaissance: The New Struggle*, ed. M.W. Makgoba [Sandton & Cape Town: Mafube & Tafelberg, 1999], pp. 184–199, especially pp. 189–191, 197), and the importance of the university as a site

for the development of culture is thus highlighted (H.W. Vilakazi, 'The Problem of African Universities', in *African Renaissance: The New Struggle*, ed. M.W. Makgoba [Sandton & Cape Town: Mafube & Tafelberg, 1999], pp. 200–209), this has not translated in practice into increased support for the humanities, as one would expect from the logic of the African Renaissance. Instead, government seems increasingly to be expecting the humanities to fit the same methodological and research agendas as the sciences, an insistence which serves to render the humanities an eternally inadequate laboratory.

CHAPTER 6 Shakespeare and the coconuts

1 Kopano Matlwa, *Coconut* (Johannesburg: Jacana Media, 2007).

2 Matlwa, *Coconut*, p. 99. Italics in the original.

3 Matlwa, *Coconut*, pp. 100–101. Italics in the original.

4 Matlwa, *Coconut*, pp. 101–103. Italics in the original.

5 Matlwa, *Coconut*, pp. 108–109. Italics in the original.

6 Matlwa, *Coconut*, pp. 108–109. Italics in the original.

7 Matlwa, *Coconut*, p. 123. Italics in the original.

8 Matlwa, *Coconut*, pp. 103, 104. Italics in the original.

9 Matlwa, *Coconut*, pp. 111–112.

10 Matlwa, *Coconut*, p. 114. Italics in the original.

11 Matlwa, *Coconut*, p. 125. Italics in the original.

12 Matlwa, *Coconut*, pp. 124, 125. Italics in the original.

13 Matlwa, *Coconut*, p. 118.

14 Matlwa, *Coconut*, p. 137. Italics in the original.

15 Matlwa, *Coconut*, p. 154. Italics in the original.

16 See Carolyn McKinney, '"If I Speak English Does it Make Me Less Black Anyway?" "Race" and English in South African Desegregated Schools', *English Academy Review* 24.2 (2007): 6–24.

17 Matlwa, *Coconut*, p. 146. Italics in the original.

18 Matlwa, *Coconut*, p. 147. Italics in the original.

19 Matlwa, *Coconut*, p. 146.

20 Matlwa, *Coconut*, p. 152. Italics in the original.

21 Matlwa, *Coconut*, pp. 152–153. Italics in the original.

22 Ngugi wa Thiong'o, *Decolonising the Mind: The Politics of Language in African Literature* (London: James Currey, 1986).

23 Rian Malan, 'Requiem for a Lonely Man', *The Sunday Independent* 16 December 2007, p. 9. Malan concludes: '[I]f it weren't for Aids, crime, unemployment, collapsing hospitals, crippled bureaucracies, Zimbabwe and the arms deal, we'd have to cast him as a great president.'

24 Malan, 'Requiem'.

25 Xolela Mangcu, *To the Brink: The State of Democracy in South Africa* (Pietermaritzburg: UKZN Press, 2008), p. 152.

26 Fiona Forde, 'No More Whispering in the Corridors, Says Zuma', *The Sunday Independent* 13 January 2008, p. 3.

27 If Mbeki is a coconut, Zuma is a chameleon, and his apparent demagoguery is belied by his ability to speak plainly to every interest group; Mbeki may be cast in the public mind as protecting the interests of the economic elite, but Zuma has not given any indication that he will threaten these interests.

28 Kevin Bloom & Phillip de Wet, 'Fear and Loathing in Polokwane: The Big Stuff', *Maverick* n.d. Accessed August 2009, http://www.maverick.co.za/ViewStory.asp?StoryID=183105.

29 Anthony Sampson's 2001 glowing assessment of Mbeki, which focuses on his 'Englishness', concludes: 'His intellectual detachment allows him to see his country in a wider context, and his love of Shakespeare is part of his understanding that Africa's problems are part of the broader problems of the human condition. With this perspective he will not be easily lured, like so many African leaders, in the direction of dictatorship.' ('President Select', *The Observer* 10 June 2001. Accessed January 2008, http://www.guardian.co.uk/world/2001/jun/10/nelsonmandela.southafrica.) The intervening years suggest Sampson had too much faith, both in Mbeki and in Shakespeare's influence. After the AIDS debacle

(very publicly informed by Mbeki's surfing), and in the face of what Mbeki's Shakespeare has come to mean, Sampson's listing of the president's interests as 'Poetry, the internet' can only draw ironic sniggers from South Africans. Given the overall tone of the article, I am sure this was not Sampson's intention.

30 Allister Sparks, 'Implications of a Zuma Presidency', *Homecoming Revolution* 28 November 2007. Accessed January 2008, http://www.homecomingrevolution.co.za/hcrblog/?p=320.

31 Isabel Hofmeyr, 'Reading Debating/Debating Reading: The Case of the Lovedale Literary Society, or Why Mandela Quotes Shakespeare', in *Africa's Hidden Histories: Everyday Literacy and Making the Self*, ed. K. Barber (Bloomington: Indiana University Press, 2006), pp. 258–277; p. 271.

32 Vukani Mde, 'Mbeki Struts and Frets His Hour upon the Stage', *Business Day* 22 February 2006. Accessed February 2009, http://www.businessday.co.za/articles/specialreports.aspx?ID=BD4A150829.

33 See Ngugi wa Thiong'o, *Decolonising the Mind*.

34 Mde, 'Mbeki Struts'.

35 *Madam & Eve*, by Stephen Francis and Rico, *Mail and Guardian* 30 November – 6 December 2007, p. 33. Permission to use the cartoon is gratefully acknowledged.

36 Natasha Distiller, *South Africa, Shakespeare and Post-colonial Culture* (Lampeter: Edwin Mellen, 2005), p. 231.

37 See Natasha Distiller, '"The Zulu Macbeth": The Value of an "African Shakespeare"', *Shakespeare Survey* 57 (2004): 159–168, p. 162.

38 See Sarah Nuttall and Cheryl-Ann Michael, eds, *Senses of Culture: South African Culture Studies* (Oxford and New York: Oxford University Press, 2000); Distiller, *South Africa*; and Mangcu, *To The Brink*, p. 9.

Bibliography

Abrahams, P. *Tell Freedom*. London: Faber and Faber, 1954.

Achebe, C. 'An Image of Africa: Racism in Conrad's *Heart of Darkness*'. In *Heart of Darkness: An Authoritative Text, Backgrounds and Sources, Criticism*, 3rd ed., ed. R. Kimbrough. London: Norton, 1988, pp. 251–261.

Ahmad, A. 'The Politics of Literary Postcoloniality'. *Race & Class* 36.3 (1995): 1–20.

Amoko, A. 'The Magistrature of English: Postcolonialism, Globalism and Literary Studies'. Unpublished paper, 'Condition of the Subject' Conference, London, July 2003.

Appiah, K.A. 'Is the "Post-" in "Postcolonial" the "Post-" in "Postmodern"?' In *Dangerous Liaisons: Gender, Nation, and Postcolonial Perspectives*, eds A. McClintock, A. Mufti, & E. Shohat. Minneapolis & London: University of Minnesota Press, 1997, pp. 420–445.

Arnold, M. *Culture and Anarchy*, ed. S. Lipman. New Haven & London: Yale University Press, 1994 [1869].

Ashcroft, B. *Post-colonial Transformation*. London & New York: Routledge, 2001.

Attwell, D. *Rewriting Modernity: Studies in Black South African Literary History*. Pietermaritzburg: UKZN Press, 2005.

Baldauf, S. 'Thabo Mbeki: The Fall of Africa's Shakespearean Figure', *Christian Science Monitor* 22 September 2008. Accessed 1 June 2011, http://www.csmonitor.com/World/Africa/2008/0922/p01s01-woaf.html.

Bate, J. 'Introduction'. In *Titus Andronicus*, ed. J. Bate. London & New York: Routledge, 1995, pp. 1–121.

Bate, J. *The Genius of Shakespeare.* London & Basingstoke: Picador, 1997.

BBC News. 'South Africa Reinstates Authors', 22 April 2001. Accessed 16 August 2005, http://news.bbc.co.uk/hi/english/entertainment/arts/newsid_1291000/1291396.stm.

Beehler, S.A. '"That's a Certain Text": Problematizing Shakespeare Instruction in American Schools and Colleges'. *Shakespeare Quarterly* 41.2 (1990): 195–205.

Bellamy, E.J. 'Psychoanalysis and the Subject in/of/for the Renaissance'. In *Reconfiguring the Renaissance: Essays in Critical Materialism*, ed. J Crewe. Lewisburg: Bucknell University Press, 1992, pp. 19–33.

Belsey, C. *The Subject of Tragedy: Identity and Difference in Renaissance Drama.* London & New York: Methuen, 1985.

Belsey, C. *Why Shakespeare?* Hampshire & New York: Palgrave Macmillan, 2007.

Bernstein, H. *The Rift: The Exile Experiences of South Africans.* London: Jonathan Cape, 1994.

Bhabha, H. *The Location of Culture.* London & New York: Routledge, 1994.

Biko, S. *I Write What I Like*, ed. A. Stubbs. London: Bowerdean, 1978.

Bloom, K. & P. de Wet. 'Fear and Loathing in Polokwane: The Big Stuff', *Maverick* n.d. Accessed August 2009, http://www.maverick.co.za/ViewStory.asp?StoryID=183105.

Boehmer, E. *Empire, the National, and the Postcolonial 1890–1920.* Oxford: Oxford University Press, 2002.

Bond, P., ed. *Fanon's Warning: A Civil Society Reader on the New Partnership for Africa's Development.* Trenton, NJ: Africa World Press, 2002.

Brantlinger, P. *Who Killed Shakespeare? What's Happened to English since the Radical Sixties.* London & New York: Routledge, 2001.

Bristol, M.D. *Shakespeare's America, America's Shakespeare.* London & New York: Routledge, 1990.

Bruster, D. 'Shakespeare and the End of History: Period as Brand Name'. In *Shakespeare and Modernity*, ed. H. Grady. London: Routledge, 2000, pp. 168–188.

Burckhardt, J. *The Civilization of the Renaissance in Italy.* London: Phaidon, 1944.

Butler, J. 'After Loss, What Then?' In *Loss: The Politics of Mourning*, eds D.L. Eng & D. Kazanjian. Berkeley: University of California Press, 2003, pp. 467–473.

Butler, J., R. Elphick, & D. Welsh. *Democratic Liberalism in South Africa: Its History and Prospects.* Middleton, CT, & Cape Town: Wesleyan University Press & David Philip, 1987.

Césaire, A. *Discourse on Colonialism*, trans. J. Pinkham. New York: Monthly Review Press, 1955; 1972.

Chanaiwa, D. 'African Humanism in Southern Africa: The Utopian, Traditionalist, and Colonialist Worlds of Mission-Educated Elites'. In *Independence Without Freedom: The*

Political Economy of Colonial Education in Southern Africa, eds A.T. Mugomba & M. Nyaggah. Oxford & Santa Barbara, CA: ABC-Clio, 1980, pp. 9–39.

Chapman, M. *Southern African Literatures*. London & New York: Longman, 1996.

Chipkin, I. *Do South Africans Exist? Nationalism, Democracy and the Identity of 'the People'*. Johannesburg: Wits University Press, 2007.

Chrisman, L. *Rereading the Imperial Romance: British Imperialism and South African Resistance in Haggard, Schreiner, and Plaatje*. Oxford: Clarendon Press, 2000.

Chrisman, L. 'Rethinking Black Atlanticism'. *Black Scholar* 30.3/4 (Fall/Winter 2000): 12–18.

Chrisman, L. 'Beyond Black Atlantic and Postcolonial Studies: The South African Differences of Sol Plaatje and Peter Abrahams'. In *Postcolonial Studies and Beyond*, eds A. Loomba, S. Kaul, M. Bunzl, A. Burton, & J. Esty. Durham & London: Duke University Press, 2005, pp. 252–271.

Cleary, S.M. 'African Renaissance: Challenges for South Africa'. In *The African Renaissance: Occasional Papers*. Johannesburg: Konrad Adenauer Stiftung, 1998, pp. 21–27.

Cloud, R. '"The Very Names of the Persons": Editing and the Invention of Dramatick Character'. In *Staging the Renaissance*, eds D. Scott Kastan & P. Stallybrass. New York & London: Routledge, 1991, pp. 88–96.

Coetzee, A. 'Justifying the Teaching of Shakespeare to ESL Learners in the Junior Secondary Phase'. MA diss., University of Potchefstroom, 1997.

Collins, M.J. 'For World and Stage: An Approach to Teaching Shakespeare'. *Shakespeare Quarterly* 41.2 (1990): 251–261.

'Comments on the Series'. Shakespeare 2000 website, n.d. Accessed April 2005, http://www.shakespeare2000.com/comments.html.

Cooppan, V. 'W(h)ither Post-colonial Studies? Towards the Transnational Study of Race and Nation'. In *Postcolonial Theory and Criticism*, eds L. Chrisman & B. Parry. Cambridge: The English Association, 2000, pp. 1–35.

Couzens, T. 'Early South African Black Writing'. In *A Celebration of Black and African Writing*, eds B. King & K. Ogungbesan. Nigeria: Ahmadu Bello University Press & Oxford University Press, 1975, pp. 1–14.

Couzens, T. *The New African: A Study of the Life and Works of H.I.E. Dhlomo*. Johannesburg: Ravan Press, 1985.

Couzens, T. 'A Moment in the Past: William Tsikinya-Chaka'. *Shakespeare in Southern Africa* 2 (1988): 60–66.

Couzens, T. 'Widening Horizons of African Literature, 1870–1900'. In *Literature and Society in South Africa*, eds L. White & T. Couzens. Cape Town: Maskew Miller Longman, 1984, pp. 60–80.

Couzens, T. & B. Willan. 'Solomon T. Plaatje, 1876–1932: An Introduction'. *English in Africa* 3.2 (1976): 1–99.

Crewe, J., ed. *Reconfiguring the Renaissance: Essays in Critical Materialism*. Lewisburg: Bucknell University Press, 1992.

Cunningham, K. 'Shakespeare, the Public, and Public Education'. *Shakespeare Quarterly* 49.3 (1998): 293–298.

Dalamba, Y. 'Towards an African Renaissance: Some Thoughts on the Renaissance Conference September 28th & 29th

1998 and its Future Implications'. *Critical Arts* 14.1 (2000): 44–72.

Daymond, M.J., D. Driver, S. Meintjies, L. Molema, C. Musengezi, M. Orford, & N. Rasebotsa, eds. *Women Writing Africa: The Southern Region.* Johannesburg: Wits University Press, 2003.

De Grazia, M. *Shakespeare Verbatim: The Reproduction of Authenticity and the 1790 Apparatus.* Oxford: Clarendon Press, 1991.

De Grazia, M. & P. Stallybrass. 'The Materiality of the Shakespearean Text'. *Shakespeare Quarterly* 44.3 (1993): 255–283.

De Kok, I. *Seasonal fires: new and selected poems.* New York: Seven Stories Press, 2006.

De Kock, L. 'English and the Colonisation of Form'. *Journal of Literary Studies* 8.1 (June 1992): 33–54.

De Kock, L. *Civilising Barbarians: Missionary Narrative and African Textual Response in Nineteenth-Century South Africa.* Johannesburg: Wits University Press, 1996.

De Kock, L. 'Sitting for the Civilization Test: The Making(s) of a Civil Imaginary in Colonial South Africa'. *Poetics Today* 22.2 (2001): 391–412.

De Kock, L. 'South Africa in the Global Imaginary: An Introduction'. In *South Africa in the Global Imaginary,* eds L. de Kock, L. Bethlehem, & S. Laden. Pretoria: Unisa Press, 2004, pp. 1–31.

Dessen, A.C. *Titus Andronicus.* Manchester & New York: Manchester University Press, 1989.

Dirlik, A. 'The Postcolonial Aura: Third World Criticism in the Age of Global Capitalism'. *Critical Inquiry* 20 (1994): 328–356.

Distiller, N. '"We're Black, Stupid": uMabatha and the New South Africa on the World Stage'. In *Under Construction: 'Race' and Identity in South Africa Today*, eds N. Distiller & M. Steyn. Cape Town: Heinemann, 2004, pp. 149–162.

Distiller, N. '"The Zulu Macbeth": The Value of an "African Shakespeare"'. *Shakespeare Survey* 57 (2004): 159–168.

Distiller, N. *South Africa, Shakespeare, and Post-colonial Culture*. Lampeter: Edwin Mellen, 2005.

Distiller, N. & M. Samuelson. '"Denying the Coloured Mother": Gender and Race in South Africa'. *L'Homme* 16.2 (2005): 28–46.

Dollimore, J. *Radical Tragedy*, 2nd ed. Hertfordshire: Harvester Wheatsheaf, 1989.

Dollimore, J. & A. Sinfield, eds. *Political Shakespeare: New Essays in Cultural Materialism*. Manchester & New York: Manchester University Press, 1985.

Driver, D. '*Drum* Magazine (1951–59) and the Spatial Configurations of Gender'. In *Text, Theory, Space: Land, Literature and History in South Africa and Australia*, eds K. Darian-Smith, L. Gunner, & S. Nuttall. London: Routledge, 1996, pp. 231–241.

Dubow, S. *Racial Segregation and the Origins of Apartheid in South Africa, 1919–36*. London: Macmillan, 1989.

Duncan, G.A. *Lovedale: Coercive Agency*. Pietermaritzburg: Cluster, 2003.

Eagleton, T. 'The Witches are the Heroines of the Piece ...' In *'Macbeth': Contemporary Critical Essays*, ed. A. Sinfield. London: Macmillan, 1992, pp. 46–52.

Eagleton, T. *Literary Theory: An Introduction*, 2nd ed. Oxford: Blackwell, 1996 [1983].

Erasmus, Z., ed. *Coloured by History, Shaped by Place: New Perspectives on Coloured Identities in Cape Town*. Cape Town: Kwela & South African History Online, 2001.

Evans, M. *Signifying Nothing: Truth's True Contexts in Shakespeare's Texts*, 2nd ed. Hertfordshire: Harvester Wheatsheaf, 1989.

Fanon, F. *The Wretched of the Earth*, trans. C. Farrington, intr. J.-P. Sartre. London: Penguin, 1961; 1990.

Fish, S. *Professional Correctness: Literary Studies and Political Change*. London & Cambridge, MA: Harvard University Press, 1995.

Foakes, R.A. *Shakespeare and Violence*. Cambridge: Cambridge University Press, 2003.

Forde, F. 'No More Whispering in the Corridors, says Zuma'. *The Sunday Independent* 13 January 2008, p. 3.

Francis, S. & Rico. *Madam & Eve*. Comic strip in *Mail & Guardian* 30 November – 6 December 2007, p. 33.

Garber, M. *Shakespeare After All*. New York: Anchor Books, 2004.

Gilmour, M., ed. *Shakespeare for All in Secondary Schools*. London: Cassell, 1996.

Grady, H. *Shakespeare's Universal Wolf: Studies in Early Modern Reification*. Oxford: Clarendon Press, 1996.

Gray, S. 'Plaatje's Shakespeare'. *English in Africa* 4.1 (1977): 1–6.

Gray, S. 'Not a Sher-fire Hit', *Mail & Guardian Online* 10 January 1997. Accessed January 2008, http://www.chico.mweb.co.za/mg/art/reviews/97jan/12jan-sher.html.

Gready, P. 'The Sophiatown Writers of the Fifties: The Unreal Reality of Their World'. *Journal of Southern African Studies* 16.1 (1990): 139–164.

Green, M. 'Translating the Nation: From Plaatje to Mpe'. *Journal of Southern African Studies* 34.2 (June 2008): 325–342.

Greenblatt, S. 1986. 'Psychoanalysis and Renaissance Culture'. In *Literary Theory/Renaissance Texts*, eds P. Parker & D. Quint. Baltimore & London: Johns Hopkins University Press, pp. 210–224.

Greenblatt, S. & G. Gunn, eds. *Redrawing the Boundaries: The Transformation of English and American Literary Studies*. New York: Modern Language Association of America, 1992.

Griffiths, G. 'The Post-colonial Project: Critical Approaches and Problems'. In *New National and Post-colonial Literatures: An Introduction*, ed. B. King. Oxford: Clarendon Press, 1996, pp. 164–177.

Harris, B. 'Sexuality as a Signifier for Power Relations: Using Lavinia, of Shakespeare's *Titus Andronicus*'. *Criticism* 38.3 (1996): 383–407.

Haupt, A. 'Identity and the Politics of Representation in Hip Hop'. In *Under Construction: 'Race' and Identity in South Africa Today*, eds N. Distiller & M. Steyn. Cape Town: Heinemann, 2004, pp. 199–209.

Hawkes, T. *Meaning by Shakespeare*. London & New York: Routledge, 1992.

Hees, E. Review of *Woza Shakespeare! 'Titus Andronicus' in South Africa*, by A. Sher & G. Doran. *South African Theatre Journal* 1 & 2 (1997): 298–304.

Hofmeyr, I. *The Portable Bunyan: A Transnational History of 'The Pilgrim's Progress'*. Princeton: Princeton University Press, 2004.

Hofmeyr, I. 'Reading Debating/Debating Reading: The Case of the Lovedale Literary Society, or Why Mandela Quotes Shakespeare'. In *Africa's Hidden Histories: Everyday Literacy and Making the Self*, ed. K. Barber. Bloomington: Indiana University Press, 2006, pp. 258–277.

Holderness, G., ed. *The Shakespeare Myth*. New York: Manchester University Press, 1988.

Holmes, J. '"A World Elsewhere": Shakespeare in South Africa'. *Shakespeare Survey* 55 (2002): 271–284.

Hooper, M. 'Nation, Narration and Cultural Translation: *Heart of Darkness* and *Mhudi*'. *Alternation* 4.2 (1997): 103–113.

Howard, J.E. 'The New Historicism in Renaissance Studies'. In *Renaissance Historicism*, eds A.F. Kinney & D.S. Collins. Amherst: University of Massachusetts Press, 1987, pp. 3–33.

Howard, T. Review of *Wozza [sic] Shakespeare! 'Titus Andronicus' in South Africa*, by A. Sher & G. Doran. *New Theatre Quarterly* 14.3 (1998): 294.

Husemeyer, L., ed. *Watchdogs or Hypocrites? The Amazing Debate on South African Liberals and Liberalism*. Johannesburg: Friedrich-Naumann-Stiftung, 1997.

IOL News. 'Malema: White People are Criminals', 8 May 2011. Accessed May 2011, http://www.iol.co.za/news/white-people-are-criminals-malema-1.1066339.

James, H. 'Cultural Disintegration in *Titus Andronicus*: Mutilating Titus, Vergil, and Rome'. In *Violence in Drama*, ed. J.M.A. Redmond. Cambridge & New York: Cambridge University Press, 1991, pp. 123–140.

Johnson, D. 'Starting Positions: The Social Functions of Literature in the Cape'. *Journal of Southern African Studies* 19.4 (1993): 615–633.

Johnson, D. *Shakespeare and South Africa*. Oxford: Clarendon Press, 1996.

Johnson, D. 'From the Colonial to the Post-colonial: Shakespeare and Education in Africa'. In *Post-colonial Shakespeares*, eds A. Loomba & M. Orkin. London & New York: Routledge, 1998, pp. 218–234.

Johnson, D. 'Lessons from Africa'. *Mail & Guardian* Beyond Matric Supplement, 7 September 2001, pp. 21–27.

Johnson, R.W. & D. Welsh, eds. *Ironic Victory: Liberalism in Post-liberation South Africa*. Oxford: Oxford University Press, 1998.

Jordan, A.C. *Towards an African Literature: The Emergence of Literary Form in Xhosa*. Berkeley, Los Angeles, & London: University of California Press, 1973.

Jordan, B.V. 'Using the English Language, South African Writers Fight Back against the Colonizers' Writings and Philosophies'. PhD diss., Albany State University, 1995.

Kahn, C. 'Remembering Shakespeare Imperially: The 1916 Tercentenary'. *Shakespeare Quarterly* 52.4 (2001): 456–478.

Karis, T. & G.M. Carter, eds. *From Protest to Challenge: A Documentary History of African Politics in South Africa 1882–1964, Volume 3: Challenge and Violence 1953–1964*. Stanford, CA: Hoover Institution Press, 1977.

Keegan, T. *Colonial South Africa and the Origins of the Racial Order*. Cape Town & Johannesburg: David Philip, 1996.

Kinney, A.F. 'Preface'. In *Renaissance Historicism*, eds A.F. Kinney & D.S. Collins. Amherst: University of Massachusetts Press, 1987, pp. viii–xv.

Kinney, A.F. & D.S. Collins, eds. *Renaissance Historicism*. Amherst: University of Massachusetts Press, 1987.

Kirkwood, M. 'The Colonizer: A Critique of the English South African Culture Theory'. In *Poetry South Africa: Selected Papers from 'Poetry 74'*, eds P. Wilhelm & J.A. Polley. Craighall: Ad. Donker, 1976, pp. 102–133.

Landsberg, C. & F. Kornegay. 'The African Renaissance: A Quest for Pax Africana and Pan-Africanism'. In *South Africa and Africa: Reflections on the African Renaissance*. Braamfontein: Foundation for Global Dialogue Occasional Paper No. 17, October 1998, pp. 16–28.

Leavis, F.R. *Education and the University: A Sketch for an 'English School'*. London: Chatto & Windus, 1943.

Lemmer, A. 'Upgrading the Study of Shakespeare in Southern African Secondary Schools: An Interim Report on the Schools' Text Project'. *Shakespeare in Southern Africa* 2 (1988): 67–77.

Lemmer, A. & J. Bursey. Introductory material to *Shakespeare's 'Macbeth'*. Manzini: Macmillan, 1994, pp. 4–6, 169–173.

Lenahan, P. 'Interacting with Shakespeare's Figurative Language: A Project in Materials Development for the L2 Classroom'. MA diss., Rhodes University, 1994.

Limb, P. 'Early ANC Leaders and the British World: Ambiguities and Identities'. *Historia* 47.1 (2002): 56–82.

Limb, P. 'Sol Plaatje Reconsidered: Rethinking Plaatje's Attitudes to Class, Nation, Gender, and Empire'. *African Studies* 62.1 (2003): 33–52.

Lloyd, D. 'Colonial Trauma/Postcolonial Recovery?' *Interventions* 2.2 (2000): 212–228.

Lodge, T. *Politics in South Africa from Mandela to Mbeki.* Cape Town: David Philip, 2002.

Loomba, A. *Gender, Race, Renaissance Drama.* New Delhi: Oxford University Press, 1992.

Loomba, A. 'Shakespearian Transformations'. In *Shakespeare and National Culture*, ed. J.J. Joughin. Manchester & New York: Manchester University Press, 1997, pp. 109–141.

Loomba, A. *Colonialism/Postcolonialism.* London & New York: Routledge, 1998.

Loomba, A. 'Local-manufacture Made-in-India Othello Fellows'. In *Post-colonial Shakespeares*, eds A. Loomba & M. Orkin. London & New York: Routledge, 1998, pp. 143–163.

Loomba, A. *Shakespeare, Race, and Colonialism.* Oxford: Oxford University Press, 2002.

MacArthur, J.H. *Critical Contexts of Sidney's 'Astrophil and Stella' and Spenser's 'Amoretti'.* Victoria, BC: English Literary Studies Monograph Series, University of Victoria, 1989.

Mack, T.L. 'What Can You Learn from a Rainbow?' *Interracial Voice*, March/April 1999. Accessed December 2008, http://www.webcom.com/~intvoice/tracy.html.

Magubane, B.M. 'The African Renaissance in Historical Perspective'. In *African Renaissance: The New Struggle*, ed. M.W. Makgoba. Sandton & Cape Town: Mafube & Tafelberg, 1999, pp. 10–36.

Mahtani, M. 'Mixed Metaphors: Positioning "Mixed Race" Identity'. In *Situating 'Race' and Racisms in Space, Time, and Theory: Critical Essays for Activists and Scholars*, eds J.-A. Lee & J. Lutz. Montreal: McGill-Queen's University Press, 2005, pp. 77–93.

Makgoba, M.W., ed. *African Renaissance: The New Struggle*. Sandton & Cape Town: Mafube & Tafelberg, 1999.

Makgoba, M.W., T. Shope, & T. Mazwai. 'Introduction'. In *African Renaissance: The New Struggle*, ed. M.W. Makgoba. Sandton & Cape Town: Mafube & Tafelberg, 1999, pp. i–xii.

Makua, A.A. 'Taking the Fear out of Shakespeare: Approaches to the Teaching of *Macbeth*'. *Educamus* (July 1989): 18–20.

Malan, R. 'Requiem for a Lonely Man'. *The Sunday Independent* 16 December 2007, p. 9.

Mamdani, M. 'There Can Be No African Renaissance Without an Africa-focussed Intelligentsia'. In *African Renaissance: The New Struggle*, ed. M.W. Makgoba. Sandton & Cape Town: Mafube & Tafelberg, 1999, pp. 125–134.

Mandela, N. *No Easy Walk to Freedom: Letters from Underground*. Oxford: Heinemann International, 1989.

Mangcu, X. *To the Brink: The State of Democracy in South Africa*. Pietermaritzburg: UKZN Press, 2008.

Mannoni, O. *Prospero and Caliban: The Psychology of Colonisation*, 2nd ed. New York: Frederick A. Praeger, 1956; 1964. First published 1950 as *Psychologie de la Colonisation*.

Manzoor, S. 'The Coconut Conundrum', *The Guardian* 30 July 2007. Accessed December 2008, http://www.sarfrazmanzoor.co.uk.

Marcus, L. 'Renaissance/Early Modern Studies'. In *Redrawing the Boundaries: The Transformation of English and American Literary Studies*, eds S. Greenblatt & G. Gunn. New York: Modern Language Association of America, 1992, pp. 41–63.

Marcus, L. *Unediting the Renaissance: Shakespeare, Marlowe, Milton*. London & New York: Routledge, 1996.

Marshall, C. '"I Can Interpret All Her Martyr'd Signs": *Titus Andronicus*, Feminism, and the Limits of Interpretation'. In *Sexuality and Politics in Renaissance Drama*, eds C. Levin & K. Robertson. Lampeter: Edwin Mellen, 1991, pp. 193–214.

Matlwa, K. 'Call me a Coconut but African Tongues are Destined for Obscurity'. *Sunday Times* 7 October 2007, p. 29.

Matlwa, K. *Coconut*. Johannesburg: Jacana Media, 2007.

Mavimbela, V. 'The African Renaissance: A Workable Dream'. In *South Africa and Africa: Reflections on the African Renaissance*. Braamfontein: Foundation for Global Dialogue Occasional Paper No. 17, October 1998, pp. 29–34.

Mbeki, T. 'The African Renaissance'. In *South Africa and Africa: Reflections on the African Renaissance*. Braamfontein: Foundation for Global Dialogue Occasional Paper No. 17, October 1998, pp. 38–41.

Mbeki, T. 'Prologue'. In *African Renaissance: The New Struggle*, ed. M.W. Makgoba. Sandton & Cape Town: Mafube & Tafelberg, 1999, pp. xiii–xxi.

Mbembe, A. 'Aesthetics of Superfluity'. *Public Culture* 16.3 (2004): 373–406.

McClaren, P. 'Traumatizing Capital: Oppositional Pedagogies in the Age of Consent'. In *Critical Education in the New Information Age*, ed. M. Castalls et al. Lanham: Rowman and Littlefield, 1999, pp. 1–36.

McClintock, A. 'The Angel of Progress: Pitfalls of the Term "Postcolonial"'. In *Colonial Discourse/Postcolonial Theory*, eds F. Barker, P. Hulme, & M. Iversen. Manchester & New York: Manchester University Press, 1994, pp. 253–266.

McKinney, C. '"If I Speak English Does it Make Me Less Black Anyway?" "Race" and English in South African Desegregated Schools'. *English Academy Review* 24.2 (2007): 6–24.

Mde, V. 'Mbeki Struts and Frets His Hour upon the Stage', *Business Day* 22 February 2006. Accessed February 2009, http://www.businessday.co.za/articles/specialreports. aspx?ID=BD4A150829.

Metz, H.G. 'Stage History of *Titus Andronicus*'. *Shakespeare Quarterly* 28.2 (1997): 154–169.

Mngxitama, A. 'Coconut Kids Have Lost Touch with Their Roots'. *City Press* 30 September 2007, p. 26.

Modisane, B. *Blame Me on History*. Craighall: Ad. Donker, 1963; 1986.

Mowat, B.A. 'Lavinia's Message: Shakespeare and Myth'. *Renaissance Papers* (1981): 55–69.

Mphahlele, E. *Down Second Avenue*. London: Faber and Faber, 1959.

Mphahlele, E. 'Prometheus in Chains: The Fate of English in South Africa'. *English Academy Review* 2.1 (1984): 89–104.

Mphahlele, E. 'Landmarks of Literary History in South Africa: A Black Perspective'. In *Perspectives on South African English Literature*, eds M. Chapman, C. Gardner, & E. Mphahlele. Craighall: Ad. Donker, 1992, pp. 37–59.

Mphahlele, E. 'An Apple for the Teachers'. *Tribute* (August 1994): 117–118.

Mugo, M.G. 'African Culture in Education for Sustainable Development'. In *African Renaissance: The New Struggle*, ed. M.W. Makgoba. Sandton & Cape Town: Mafube & Tafelberg, 1999, pp. 210–232.

Mullineux, P. 'An Examination of the Use of the Contextual Question in Examining Shakespeare's Plays at the Standard Ten Level in Cape Education Department Schools'. MA diss., Rhodes University, 1988.

Mzamane, M.V. 'Culture and Social Environment in the Pre-colonial Era'. *Tydskrif vir Letterkunde* 46.1 (2009): 192–205.

New Zimbabwe News. 'Malema v BBC Journalist', 8 April 2010. Accessed May 2011, http://www.newzimbabwe.com/news/news.aspx?newsID=2201.

Ngugi wa Thiong'o. *Decolonising the Mind: The Politics of Language in African Literature*. London: James Currey, 1986.

Ngugi wa Thiong'o. *Moving the Centre: The Struggle for Cultural Freedoms*. London: James Currey, 1993.

Nicol, M. *A Good-looking Corpse*. London: Secker & Warburg, 1991.

Noble, L. '"And Make Two Pasties of Your Shameful Heads": Medicinal Cannibalism and Healing the Body Politic in *Titus Andronicus*'. *ELH* 70 (2003): 677–708.

Ntuli, P.P. 'The Missing Link between Culture and Education: Are We Still Chasing Gods that Are Not Our Own?' In *African Renaissance: The New Struggle*, ed. M.W. Makgoba. Sandton & Cape Town: Mafube & Tafelberg, 1999, pp. 184–199.

Nuttall, S. & C.-A. Michael, eds. *Senses of Culture: South African Culture Studies*. Oxford & New York: Oxford University Press, 2000.

Oboe, A. 'Of Books and The Book: The Evangelical Mission in South African Literature'. In *Colonies – Missions – Cultures – in the English-speaking World*, ed. G. Stilz. Tubingen: Stauffenburg Verlag, 2001, pp. 235–246.

O'Brien, P. 'Doing Shakespeare: "Yo! A Hit! A Very Palpable Hit!"' *English Journal* 82.4 (1993): 40–45.

Orkin, M. *Shakespeare Against Apartheid*. Craighall: Ad. Donker, 1987.

Orkin, M. 'Shakespeare and the Politics of "Unrest"'. *English Academy Review* 8 (1991): 85–97.

Orkin, M. 'The Politics of Editing the Shakespeare Text in South Africa'. *Current Writing* 5.1 (1993): 48–59.

Orkin, M. 'Re-presenting *The Tempest* in South Africa (1955–90)'. *Shakespeare in Southern Africa* 6 (1993): 45–60.

Orkin, M. 'Whose Things of Darkness? Reading/Representing *The Tempest* in South Africa after April 1994'. In

Shakespeare and National Culture, ed. J.J. Joughin. Manchester & New York: Manchester University Press, 1997, pp. 142–170.

Orkin, M. 'Possessing the Book and Peopling the Text'. In *Post-colonial Shakespeares*, eds A. Loomba & M. Orkin. London & New York: Routledge, 1998, pp. 186–204.

Orkin, M. 'Whose *Muti* in the Web of It? Seeking "Post"-colonial Shakespeare'. *Journal of Commonwealth Literature* 33.2 (1998): 15–37.

Paton, J. 'A Pleasurable Pathway to the Works of Shakespeare'. *The Daily News* 25 February 1993, p. 23.

Pechey, G. 'Post-apartheid Narratives'. In *Colonial Discourse/ Postcolonial Theory*, eds F. Barker, P. Hulme, & M. Iverson. Manchester & New York: Manchester University Press, 1994, pp. 151–171.

Pechey, G. 'Epiphanies of Africa in South African Literature'. *Pretexts: Literary and Cultural Studies* 11.1 (2002): 9–25.

Peterson, B. *Monarchs, Missionaries and African Intellectuals: African Theatre and the Unmaking of Colonial Marginality*. Johannesburg: Wits University Press, 2000.

Peterson, B. 'Sol Plaatje's *Native Life in South Africa*: Melancholy Narratives, Petitioning Selves and the Ethics of Suffering'. *The Journal of Commonwealth Literature* 43 (2008): 79–95.

Pieterse, E. & F. Meintjies, eds. *Voices of the Transition*. Johannesburg: Heinemann, 2003.

Plaatje, S. *Mhudi*, ed. T. Couzens. Broadway: Quagga, 1975.

Pratt, M.L. *Imperial Eyes: Travel Writing and Transculturation*. London: Routledge, 1992.

Pratt, M.L. 'Transculturation and Autoethnography: Peru, 1615/1980'. In *Colonial Discourse/Postcolonial Theory*, eds F. Barker, P. Hulme, & M. Iversen. Manchester & New York: Manchester University Press, 1994, pp. 24–46.

Quince, R. *Shakespeare in South Africa: Stage Productions during the Apartheid Era*. New York: Peter Lang, 2000.

Rhodes, N. *Shakespeare and the Origins of English*. Oxford: Oxford University Press, 2004.

Ricci, D. 'Titus Topples into the "Relevant" Pit'. *Shakespeare in Southern Africa* 8 (1995): 81–82.

Rich, P.B. *White Power and the Liberal Conscience: Racial Segregation and South African Liberalism, 1921–60*. Manchester: Manchester University Press, 1984.

Rose, J. *States of Fantasy*. Oxford: Clarendon Press, 1996.

Royster, F. 'White-Limed Walls: Whiteness and Gothic Extremism in Shakespeare's *Titus Andronicus*'. *Shakespeare Quarterly* 51.4 (2000): 432–455.

Saayman, W.A. *A Man with a Shadow: The Life and Times of Professor Z.K. Matthews*. Pretoria: Unisa Press, 1996.

Said, E. *Culture and Imperialism*. New York: Vintage, 1993.

Salomone, R.E. & J.E. Davis, eds. *Teaching Shakespeare into the Twenty-first Century*. Athens: Ohio University Press, 1997.

Salusbury, T. & D.H. Foster. 'Rewriting WESSA Identity'. In *Under Construction: 'Race' and Identity in South Africa Today*, eds N. Distiller & M. Steyn. Johannesburg: Heinemann, 2004, pp. 93–109.

Sampson, A. *Drum: A Venture into the New Africa*. London: Collins, 1956.

Sampson, A. 'O, What Men Dare Do', *The Observer* 22 April 2001. Accessed June 2001, http://www.observer.co.uk/comment/story/0,6903,476514,00.html.

Sampson, A. 'President Select', *The Observer* 10 June 2001. Accessed January 2008, http://www.guardian.co.uk/world/2001/jun/10/nelsonmandela.southafrica.

San Juan, Jr, E. *Beyond Postcolonial Theory*. London: Macmillan, 1999.

Sanders, M. *Complicities: The Intellectual and Apartheid*. Pietermaritzburg: UKZN Press, 2002.

Saunders, W. 'Mastering English'. *Reality* (March/April 1992): 15–16.

Saunders, W. *Shakespeare's 'Macbeth' in Modern English*. Parklands: Shakespeare 2000/Jacklin, 2001.

Scarry, E. *The Body in Pain: The Making and Unmaking of the World*. New York & Oxford: Oxford University Press, 1985.

Schalkwyk, D. 'Portrait and Proxy: Representing Plaatje and Plaatje Represented'. *Scrutiny 2* 4.2 (1999): 14–29.

Schalkwyk, D. 'Hamlet's Dreams'. *Social Dynamics* 32.2 (2006): 1–21.

Schalkwyk, D. & L. Lapula. 'Solomon Plaatje, William Shakespeare, and the Translations of Culture'. *Pretexts: Literary and Cultural Studies* 9.1 (2000): 9–26.

Scott Kastan, D. *Shakespeare and the Book*. Cambridge: Cambridge University Press, 2001.

Seddon, Deborah. 'Shakespeare's Orality: Solomon Plaatje's Setswana Translations'. *English Studies in Africa* 47.2 (2004): 77–95.

Serote, M.W. 'The African Renaissance Social Movement'. *New Agenda* 4 (2001): 51–55.

Shakespeare, W. *Shakespeare's Macbeth*, eds A. Lemmer & J. Bursey. Manzini: Macmillan, 1994.

Shakespeare, W. *Macbeth*, ed. N. Bakker, B. Mosala, A. Parr & L. Singh. Cape Town: Maskew Miller Longman, 1996.

Shakespeare, W. *Macbeth*. Wits Schools Shakespeare edition, eds H. Davis, P. Farrands, & J. Parmenter. Cape Town: Nasou Via Afrika, 2007.

Sharma, N. 'Rotten Coconuts and Other Strange Fruits', *Samar* 14 (Fall/Winter 2001). Accessed January 2008, http://www.samarmagazine.org/archive/article.php?id=62.

Shava, P.V. *A People's Voice: Black South African Writing in the Twentieth Century*. London: Zed and Ohio State University Press, 1989.

Sher, A. *The Feast*. London: Little, Brown, 1998.

Sher, A. *Beside Myself: An Autobiography*. London: Hutchinson, 2000.

Sher, A. & G. Doran. *Woza Shakespeare!: Titus Andronicus in South Africa*. London: Methuen, 1996.

Shole, S.J. 'Shakespeare in Setswana: An Evaluation of Raditladi's *Macbeth* and Plaatje's *Diphosophoso*'. *Shakespeare in Southern Africa* 4 (1990/1): 51–64.

Sinfield, A. 'Give an Account of Shakespeare and Education, Showing Why You Think They are Effective and What You Have Appreciated about Them. Support Your Comments with Precise References'. In *Political Shakespeare: New Essays in Cultural Materialism*, eds J. Dollimore &

A. Sinfield. Manchester & New York: Manchester University Press, 1985, pp. 134–157.

Sinfield, A. '*Macbeth*: History, Ideology and Intellectuals'. In '*Macbeth*': *Contemporary Critical Essays*, ed. A. Sinfield. London: Macmillan, 1992, pp. 121–136.

Sinfield, A., ed. '*Macbeth*': *New Casebooks*. London: Macmillan, 1992.

Slemon, S. 'Post-colonial Critical Theories'. In *New National and Post-colonial Literatures: An Introduction*, ed. B. King. Oxford: Clarendon Press, 1996, pp. 178–197.

Smith, M.E. 'Spectacles of Torment in *Titus Andronicus*'. *SEL* 36 (1996): 315–331.

Sole, K. 'Democratising Culture and Literature in a "New South Africa": Organisation and Theory'. *Current Writing* 62.2 (1994): 1–37.

Sole, K. 'South Africa Passes the Posts'. *Alternation* 4.1 (1997): 116–151.

Sole, K. 'Class, Continuity and Change in Black South African Literature, 1948–1960'. In *Labour, Townships and Protest: Studies in the Social History of the Witwatersrand*, ed. B. Bozzoli. Johannesburg: Ravan Press, 2001, pp. 143–182.

Soyinka, W. 'Shakespeare and the Living Dramatist'. In *Art, Dialogue and Outrage: Essays on Literature and Culture*. Ibadan: New Horn Press, 1988.

Sparks, A. 'Implications of a Zuma Presidency', *Homecoming Revolution* 28 November 2007. Accessed January 2008, http://www.homecomingrevolution.co.za/hcrblog/?p=320.

Spivak, G.C. 'Remembering the Limits: Difference, Identity and Practice'. In *Socialism and the Limits of Liberalism*, ed. P. Osborne. London & New York: Verso, 1991, pp. 227–240.

The Star. 'Malema's Millions', *The Star* 19 February 2010. Accessed May 2011, http://www.iol.co.za/news/politics/pics-malema-s-millions-1.473967.

Stein, P. & R. Jacobson, eds. *Sophiatown Speaks*. Johannesburg: Bertrams Avenue, 1986.

Steyn, M. *Whiteness Just Isn't What It Used To Be: White Identity in a Changing South Africa*. Albany: State University of New York Press, 2001.

Sunday Times. 'How Malema Made His Millions', 21 February 2010. Accessed May 2011, http://www.timeslive.co.za/sundaytimes/article318330.ece/How-Malema-made-his-millions.

Sunday Times. 'Keeping SA Schools Safe from Literature', n.d. Accessed 16 August 2005, http://www.suntimes.co.za/education/setworks/index.asp.

Taylor, G. *Reinventing Shakespeare: A Cultural History from the Restoration to the Present*. Oxford: Oxford University Press, 1989.

Themba, C. 'Through Shakespeare's Africa'. *New African* 2.8 (1963): 150–154.

Thurman, C. 'Sher and Doran's *Titus Andronicus* (1995): Importing Shakespeare, Exporting South Africa'. *Shakespeare in Southern Africa* 18 (2006): 29–36.

Tomaselli, K.G. 'Cultural Studies and Renaissance in Africa: Recovering Praxis'. *Scrutiny 2* 4.2 (1999): 43–48.

Vale, P. & S. Maseko. 'South Africa and the African Renaissance'. In *South Africa and Africa: Reflections on the African Renaissance*. Braamfontein: Foundation for Global Dialogue Occasional Paper No. 17, October 1998, pp. 2–15.

Vaughan, V.M. 'The Construction of Barbarism in *Titus Andronicus*'. In *Race, Ethnicity, and Power in the Renaissance*, ed. J.G. MacDonald. Madison, NJ, & London: Associated University Presses, 1997, pp. 165–180.

Vilakazi, H.W. 'The Problem of African Universities'. In *African Renaissance: The New Struggle*, ed. M.W. Makgoba. Sandton & Cape Town: Mafube & Tafelberg, 1999, pp. 200–209.

Vilakazi, H.W. 'The African Renaissance'. *New Agenda* 4 (2001): 56–67.

Viswanathan, G. *Masks of Conquest: Literary Study and British Rule in India*. New York: Columbia University Press, 1989.

Waetjen, T. & G. Mare. 'Tradition's Desire: The Politics of Culture in the Rape Trial of Jacob Zuma'. *Concerned Africa Scholars Bulletin* 84 (2010): 52–61.

Walters, P.S. & V. England. *The Teaching of English Literature in Black High Schools*. Grahamstown: ISEA, Rhodes University, 1988.

White, H. *Tropics of Discourse: Essays in Cultural Criticism*. Baltimore & London: Johns Hopkins University Press, 1978.

Widdowson, P., ed. *Re-reading English*. London & New York: Methuen, 1982.

Willan, B. 'Sol T. Plaatje and Tswana Literature: A Preliminary Survey'. In *Literature and Society in South Africa*, eds

L. White & T. Couzens. Cape Town: Maskew Miller Longman, 1984, pp. 81–100.

Willan, B., ed. *Sol Plaatje: Selected Writings*. Johannesburg: Wits University Press, 1996.

Williams, R. *Modern Tragedy*. Stanford, CA: Stanford University Press, 1966.

Willis, D. '"This Gnawing Vulture": Revenge, Trauma Theory, and *Titus Andronicus*'. *Shakespeare Quarterly* 53.1 (2002): 21–52.

Wilson, M. & L. Thompson, eds. *The Oxford History of South Africa, Volume 2*. Oxford: Clarendon Press, 1975.

Woeber, C. 'Error in the Religious Equation: Images of St Peter's School in South African Autobiography'. *English Academy Review* 12 (1995): 58–69.

Woeber, C. 'The Contribution of St. Peter's School to Black South African Autobiography'. PhD diss., University of the Witwatersrand, 2000.

Wynne-Davies, M. '"The Swallowing Womb": Consumed and Consuming Women in *Titus Andronicus*'. In *Shakespeare's Tragedies*, ed. S. Zimmerman. New York: St. Martin's Press, 1998, pp. 212–236.

Yogev, M. 'How Shall We Find the Concord of this Discord? Teaching Shakespeare in Israel, 1994'. *Shakespeare Quarterly* 46.1 (1995): 157–164.

Young, R. 'Hybridism and the Ethnicity of the English'. In *Cultural Readings of Imperialism: Edward Said and the Gravity of History*, eds K.A. Pearson, B. Parry, & J. Squires. New York: St. Martin's Press, 1997, pp. 127–150.

Young, R. *Postcolonialism: A Very Short Introduction*. Oxford: Oxford University Press, 2003.

Young, S. '"Let Your Indulgence Set Me Free": Reflections on an "Africanised" *Tempest* and its Implications for Critical Practice'. *Social Dynamics* 36.2 (June 2010): 315–327.

Index

Printed and bound by CPI Group (UK) Ltd, Croydon, CR0 4YY

09/06/2025

14685816-0001